IDENTITY IN SHADES

Urban Poetry and Soul

Shamir Kali Griffin

January 1, 2013

Shamirkali.com

ISBN: 1515091341
ISBN 13: 9781515091349
Library of Congress Control Number: **XXXXX (If applicable)**
LCCN Imprint Name: **City and State (If applicable)**

Table of Contents

Foreword

Shamir Kali Griffin is an accomplished scholar, noted author, and most importantly as I know him, a friend. A true friend he is indeed, a gentle soul in a seven-foot-two-inch frame. Tall One, as I affectionately call him, has been in my life for the past two years. I've seen him in hard times, poor health, and relationships that left him tattered and torn, but through all his trials, he has remained triumphant and risen with a mind-set to conquer ever-greater heights. Shamir's writing isn't transparent; it speaks from his soul and his experiences and reflects those around him that he has encountered along the way.

Having to grow up in the disadvantaged neighborhoods of Oakland and Stockton, California, he has struggled with the harsh realities that society reflects on the stereotypical black male. Though his road has not been an easy one, Shamir has managed to remain grounded and pursue his dreams despite the trials he has faced in adversity. The truth and feeling behind most of Shamir's pieces are genuine and relatable so that any man or woman can identify with them, whether gay or straight, and of any race, creed, or religious belief. His writing embodies his true character—who he is, where he once was, and where he plans to be.

Joushya Cole

Chapter I: Identity in Society and Culture

We often identify ourselves by associating who we are with a group of people in some form or another—through racial, ethnic, religious, or political categories and, in the case of gangs, environmental ones. How these identities are carried over from one aspect of our lives to another varies considerably. We must often come to question how these groups we assign ourselves to, or ones that others assign us to, affect how we carry ourselves. Are we by definition similar to one another yet different in the same sense? Does being Catholic and Brazilian differ from being an Irish Catholic? At what point do these things converge? Consider for a second who you associate yourself with. What are the benefits and negative side effects of this association?

The color violet is often associated with ambiguity, extravagance, and unconventionality. So the poetry you will read has some things that may appear to be ambiguous to you at first glance. If you let the extravagant nature of some of the works or wording settle in, you will be exposed to many more things in this world.

My last and final request is that you embrace whatever thoughts come from reading this section and let them neither flee nor linger. Some of the poems tackle issues of violence, racial discrimination, and institutional reform and may excite thoughts and feelings within you.

The Song the Ghetto Bird* Sings

Large fists pound on apartment doors.
Colored shoes scurry across the floors.
The voice of an officer demanding the door to open
As he forces himself against the protest of children.

The song that the ghetto bird sings
With loud knocks replacing friendly doorbell rings.

A woman who pleads for them not to enter
As they push their gun butts into her.
They search empty hallways and unoccupied rooms
Only to unearth a buried youth; premature tombs.

The song that the ghetto bird sings
Are funeral songs the mother sings.

A sixteen-year-old boy who is thin in frame
Is weighted down by responsibility and gang name.
Parents who sacrificed themselves to pay for school books
Now must reexamine their children's lives, second looks.

Ghetto bird is American slang for *helicopter.*

Urban Flow-etry

I spit words like bullets guaranteed to affect your vitality
Over issues that give birth to enlightenment and death to hostility.
Now humble yourself in this battle or spiritual warfare,
While others sell their souls to stay on government welfare.

Be wary of your surroundings, and if need be, hide yourself in the trenches
As cowardice and fear lead to hesitation and preemptive actions; flinches.
City nights become filled with the voices of activists
And mothers of gang members who are now childless.

This is urban poetry that is made rhythmic with baritone voices
And careful Poetic Justice–inspired choices.
It is contagious and offers words of spiritual warmth and wisdom,
But it is so raw that it needs not magnum-based protection.

I spit words like bullets guaranteed to affect your vitality
Over issues that give birth to enlightenment and death to hostility.
Now humble yourself in this battle or spiritual warfare,
While others sell their souls to stay on government welfare.

The Song of My City

The song of my city is not a quiet one.
It's the sound you hear on the ten o'clock news,
The sound you hear when a new face has been born into a family,
The loud sound of the bass being made by police knocking on the door.

The rising voices of women at Black churches filling the air
With hymns of David speaking in tongues while their daughters
Go into rapture with young boys trying to become men;
Turning away from God to enjoy temporary moments of glorified sin.

The song of my city is brought to you by migrant workers doing their best,
Of native people who stood tall in the lands of their mothers being pushed west.
The lyrics to my city had been revised and brought back by a lost generation,
Black Panthers unified by institutionalized discrimination, leaving inspiration.

My city's beats kill, fueled by thousands of local artist hungry to earn a mil.
The sound of my city was labeled *unimportant* and *whack*, strongly correlated
With the government flooding its streets with Uncle Sam–quality crack.
It is music that blows through you and rips, like bodies shot dead, buried in crypts.

A song like bullets fired six times onto empty streets.
As homeboys run bodies piling up, hearts afraid to skip beats.
The world heard this song and has waited for it to become quiet.
Though I've let you hear the prelude, I'm afraid you haven't heard a minute of it.

Winter in Oakland

Bare trees scratch at the sky with their dark branches
Like strokes of a brush painting Black hands hungry for liberation.
Autumn leaves are pushed away by winter's coming gale.

The strange sound of blood and urine pitter-pattering on the streets of Oakland,
Sounds of domestic violence proven by unclaimed bodies left in the open.
The people become victims of the bystander effect as bodies fall like hail.

Shots are poured up, and shots are fired off.
More bodies pile up over different-colored cloth.
Flashing lights of the holiday season, dyed red and blue.

*El Norteno y el Sureno,** variance among color and direction, is murder's reason.
Youth caught up, shot up, and locked up for their associated neighborhoods.
Teachers like preachers offer hope for the masses, only to be stabbed after classes.

Are we leaves falling from trees waiting for the wind to pick us up on a last thrill?
Are we the ones who turn blind eyes, self-sedated by the availability of a pill?
Trees become filled with new life, and the masses remain ignorant to this strife.

*El Norteno y el Sureno are Spanish for *the Northerner* and *the Southerner.*

Stockton

Now according to *Forbes* magazine, we are the worst American city.
Now it may be due to our lack of Anglo cuisine or increased poverty.
In my eyes, Stockton is more than just a place where old and young bodies lie.
It's where both *paleteros* and ice-cream men give us frozen treats on which we rely.

To me Stockton is Labor Day Powwows at a pillar of education, UOP.
It's Greek, Japanese, and Filipino Barrio Fiesta embracing our diversity.
It's being an IB student at Franklin to heading south to become an Edison Viking.
It's cruising around town wild and free with our friends, playing music of our liking.

We offer unique stores and restaurants from 8th street to 8 mile.
Come take a stroll with us in our shoes to that artistic place called Miracle Mile.
Come dance *Cumbias* at Flamingo to Touché where we create new lingo.
We spend time at both Delta and Kaplan College, standing on SUSD knowledge.

Yes no one wants to be "Stuck in Stockton"; the numbers 209 we stay representing.
Yet check through our Facebook pages; there simply isn't enough in a check-in.
We are victims and perpetrators of institutionalized violence fed in adolescence,
But to deny us the value of our identity would be to rob us of common sense.

Bakersfield

The wind whispers secrets to the trees
As bodies become earthbound as the leaves.
When venturing forth into the concrete jungle,
We are left with hit-and-run reminders of a driver's fumble.

People litter the sidewalks with ads of car-wash services
While morticians and lawyers assess the damages.
People in humble and vain spirits hunt for a new job
But worry as others stare and attempt to rob.

The city light illuminates dark skies on First Fridays
With eventful reminders decorated to capture gaze.
A conservative city rich in oil fields and agriculture
Still fights over disputes of whose is the better culture.

Youth attend colleges from Cal State to BC.
Others get shipped off overseas to defend democracy.
Ghetto birds fly throughout lower-income areas,
And I am reminded of home in the Bay Area.

The Silence in Gunshots

Loud, thunderous shots, explosive like fire,
Indiscriminately kill youths based on colored attire.
Gun down pedestrians, fathers, and friends in cross fire,
Clipping lives short before given the chance to retire.

There are those who are slain
Due to neighborhood affiliation or a gang.
Then there are those who try and stop fights,
Who lose their last precious heartbeat to protect someone else that night.

There are those like Edgar "Camarón" and Michael,
Whose lives were taken away by an ungodly archangel,
Leaving policemen unable to find their killers due to gunshot angles.
Beautiful God created living sculptures now lifeless as their hands dangle.

The silence in gunshots is the quietness at funerals:
It's angry friends seeking revenge, pissing on this lesson as if a urinal.
Of weeping cousins and mothers not wanting to leave their baby's memorial.
Most of all, it is the silence of knowing that you kept quiet for sake of indifference.

She Used to Be

She used to be anyone's crown jewel.
Now she relies on being anyone's tool.
She used to watch as gentlemen's car doors open.
Now her only trick was to let her legs pry open.

She relies on the sinful throws of Eve,
Hanging out with different guys, Miguel, Rick, and Steve.
She prayed for drug wounds to swiftly close.
Wanted a new life but still performed acts in old panty hose.

She used to be the woman girls admired,
The one that boys becoming men desired.
Now she is simply painted blue and black with bruises,
Over the intolerance and trespasses of affectionate strangers' misuses.

He says he beats her up to tenderize her meat,
So as she laid helpless her flesh he could then eat.
She used to be a daughter, a sister, a cousin to some and a friend to more,
But when most people see her all they see is the same town whore.

It's Sad When (A Girl Growing Up in Stockton)

It's sad when the only support you receive is from your bra,
When your boyfriend says he loves you, so you let him fuck raw.
It's sad when plans of eternity discussed over phone calls
Have left you sad and lonely, experiencing love withdrawals.

It's sad when the only test you were expected to pass was confirming pregnancy,
When others expected that a barrage of bullets would shorten your life expectancy.
It's sad when the place you live is called a house and not a home,
So you turn to the streets for shelter and roam.

It's sad when you're depicted as another girl from Stockton,
Worst city in the United States says *Forbes*, and you're checked in.
It's sad that no one expects better of you, but you know,
Just know that there is always someone else to turn to.

It's sad when you push yourself hard over economic and gender-based hurdles,
Yet you are steadily reminded by those around you of how you should just settle.
It's sad when you are one of a large group of friends to leave all this and graduate.
Only to be torn down behind the scenes by the crabs-in-the-bucket mentality, their hate.

Identity in Shades

I am of mixed ancestral and cultural identity,
But it is through dark skin I find others defining me.
I shall take this time to stand tall in my richness of creed and not lament.
To show you why God painted me black, leaving me a foundation like cement.

I am birthed on the bosoms of Oakland and Stockton,
Told that my skin color resembles coal, not copper or tin.
But it is through societal pressures beating hard on me that I become a diamond.
I make myself a testimony to defy societal views of a Black man.

Now I have never passed for anything else ex-colored man, James Weldon Johnson;
But much like "Shiny," my brilliance and intellect define and illuminate me.
Even when people tell me that the reflection of my skin is a cursed ancestry,
They say poisonous things like, "If you weren't Black, together we could be."

I flock to this like a crow in groups being called a *murder* over this ignorance.
While they stare at me wondering why my head is held high, not low in repentance.
I am shores of the Ivory Coast held captive to European profitable greed.
I am spoken word and proverb, Maya Angelou, and Langston Hughes's poetry.

My skin color and those of my brethren come in many hues and shades,
From charcoal-black deepness and colored eyes to passing tones of beige.
My skin and people are not criminal though they are being enforced by statistics
Made with white flight and decrease in education funds for prison politics.

I am that Black Boy and an American *Native Son* by Richard Wright.
I am happily walking home down allies unarmed but still a woman's fright.
I am David Chappell funny and Alice Walker creative.
My people and I were implanted here as foreigners, not native.

It is a pity to hear them say, "Black people pillage, rape, and steal."
We are descendants of a displaced people whose culture they attempted to kill.
We are hard workers both post- and preslavery,
Soldiers decorated with Medals of Honor and Valor for their bravery.

I am of mixed ancestry and cultural identity,
But it is mainstream culture that incorrectly judges me.
I am black hands striving and hungry for a higher education,
Waiting patiently for the day when my poetry will become an ignorance vaccination!

Oakland

Graffiti splashed over the concrete walls of soul and heritage
Paint images and tapestries of east-side residents without language.
Thirty-degree winds serve as frigid reminders of bay breeze,
Of cold streets that they must navigate in strange company.

Like a barrage of bullets fired into a crowd unexpectedly,
I am in shock as to where I stand in relation to my city.
I am a foreigner and a bastard to my city's cold eyes,
A stray ejaculated sperm shot into Stockton's womb, disenfranchised.

I walk the alleyways of 106th and Bancroft like a ghost trapped in memory
As I find vacant spots were plum trees once thrived and plant seeds in reverie.
I am a child who is placed under geographical joint custody,
Returning only here when there is a family-founded party.

Grandpa's Skin

Grandpa's skin is golden brown with yellow patches of wisdom.
As he sits quietly, eyes of ninety years' experiences are relaxing.
Grandfather's skin is both tight and filled with wrinkles,
Lines of time-drawn maps on elder skin and hidden dimples.

Grandfather hailed from the south and left family lands,
Started his own business and family with his two hands.
He laid fourteen seeds that spawned eight males and six beautiful girls;
Though it put a strain on him, they were his precious black pearls.

Grandfather Thomas led his family to Oakland for a new life.
He stood tall and proud in the face of adversity, even at the loss of his wife.
Grandpa's fist taught his sons virtue and how to fight,
Gave caution to young daughters of what danger looks like.

Thomas Griffin is my grandfather and I his grandson,
Standing a bit over seven feet, fed on past stories of my kin.
Though I am not the closest or similar to him,
I, like my cousins, all proudly wear Grandpa's skin.

Barbershops (Ode to R Spot)

Black hands craft graphic images, skillful yet sturdy like a surgeon,
While children of mixed heritage take in wisdom on how to be men.
Life lessons and stories bitter with history and chased with sweet laughter
Like sweet urban candy wrapped in a hood and barrio-colored wrapper.

Smells of hairspray and shaving cream mix and stick to the apron of the employees.
They line up boys with fades as they prepare for festivities and others to go overseas.
These combinations of skin in varying shades sculpt people into an enclave.
At this barbershop, there is more than a simple sense of unity.
It is a firm backbone to this Bakersfield community.

6 Times

My heart was broken six times throughout a very short time span.
I heard a loud and thunderous voice denounce me louder than a jazz band.
I was told six times to leave the place I had resided in, my father's home.
I could not and did not belong, so into the arms of strangers and the streets I roam.
You taught me how love is nothing more but purely conditional,
Messages of worthlessness and hate repeating themselves in my head: subliminal!

You will never know how much the first time had damaged me incredibly,
When I was your only son and with my mother's presence you helped birth me.
I cried for you nonstop for several days when you fell several floors down,
Then in your anger you accused me of using that time to fool around.
You relied on biblical scripture and inebriation on liquor
To remind me to hurry up and leave your house quicker.

Then you would tell me to come back and stay,
That this wasn't a problem so easily thrown away.
So I would return, and in this I learned to not go back
Because no matter how much I returned, I was thrown back.
You told me that due to sodomy I was hell destined with an infection of HIV,
And I learned that no place was home, just temperamental inconsistency.

You simply cannot see how much your hate has impacted me.
It's the reason why I don't trust compliments or the word *love* from any man.
It's inclusive of male suitors, role models, teachers, and my fraternity brothers,
All of whom have praised me and showered me with unique compliments.
Yet these things are empty, as you have sown in seeds of hate, not self-confidence.
As you look at me, Father, know that I cannot receive love from all the acts above.

God's Eyes

"Hatred stirs up strife, but love covers all sins." (Prov. 10:12)
It is this belief in scripture all of humanity should dwell.
I wonder what it is that God can see
When his children love blindly and hate selectively?

"The lord is merciful and gracious…abounding in mercy." (Psalm. 105:8)
Why do those who claim to know him select differences to hate
I wonder, what is it that our righteous God feels
When past victims discourage equality and vote yes on Prop 8 bill?

"Love suffers long and is kind: love does not envy." (1Corinthians 13:4,7)
So if love is all these things, then why is love denying access to heaven?
I wonder, what is it that God envisioned in his eyes and values
When his children sell their souls for increased market revenue?

"But as for me, I will walk with integrity." -Psalm 26:11
As through righteousness in deed and meek in mind, I pave my road to heaven.
For to me, God's eyes may see far past all of divinity and Christianity
And are crying; for instead of loving, we embrace hate and stupidity.

A Chip on My Shoulder

If you see me solely for my sexuality, you gain an inability.
You blind yourself and avoid truly seeing me.
This is a chip that was wrongfully placed on my shoulder.
Words of ignorance from society magnifies it bolder.

Can someone please explain to me this contradiction?
Why a man can be a hero when he returns from jail,
But I am labeled a faggot, destination hell?
Explain to me, please explain to me, why my associated death is HIV?

Why is it that God is praised by both rappers and conservative Christian people,
Who appear narrow minded and look at me through narrower lenses, peepholes.
When I, much like them, give both lyric and aid to needy, impoverished people
Only to be reminded that I stand a member of a partially marginalized people.

I am blessed to love without a sense of ambiguity
And cursed to know how society views and represents me.
I daily push my boulder diligently up a capitol hill,
Not unlike Sisyphus for the killing of a Prop 8 bill.

Tell me why straight men fear befriending me due to my sexual preference,
Yet I am made their proof to dispel ignorance, their bi-friend reference.
Yes I am a member of a team called bisexuality; I am love in the form duality.
So damn right, you better fear me when you incorrectly identify me!

Yes on Prop 8

Yes on Prop 8 was intended to protect the family structure.
The bill promotes natural heterosexual family unity instead of fracture.
To uphold strong, traditional American values we should abide by,
But what the bill did was marginalize a people with a lie.

The Black community, predominately Christian in its nature,
Fought hard to suppress a right that was once openly denied to her.
When our women and men were force bred but relied on jumping the broom
For the unification of our disenfranchised families but buried that history in a tomb.

KYCC said that homosexual parents lack the ability to raise or be part of a family.
Yet are we not members of brothers and sisters placed in family categories?
We grow up in shattered homes and those with both of our parents,
But this evidence is criminally erased like gunshot-residue fingerprints.

Yes on Prop 8 swore to protect church-sanctioned marriage and its divinity,
But what good is their marriage when divorce rates are 50 percent consistently?
When fathers leave wives, when domestic violence takes lives,
But yes on Prop 8 focused on us and told our equality, "Good-bye."

Black Dreams

Will someone paint for me a Black child's dream?
Who will knit in love and wisdom both delicate and strong into the seam?
Are these children, who are birthed inside of a Black woman's womb,
Left to be told that their dreams are less important than those of other dreamers?

Who will teach these dreamers when to feel hurt and when to make a fist?
When 72 percent of Black children are born to homes of single mothers left fatherless?
Are these children only allowed to dream the dreams of rapper, actor, and sports
While being pushed out of higher education and the glorification of going to courts?

Who will teach the dirty ghetto kids, strong figure, color from black to copper,
That the words *nigga* and *bitch* demean us and that this is not proper?
Who will show these dreamers that you can still, with much effort, paint a rainbow
Even if your color is called *ugly* because it is not fair as freshly fallen snow?

A Country of Heroes

We are a country of heroes, of men and women defending our rights.
We are a country of heroes, of marines, navy SEALs, army men, and restless nights.
From separate and different cultural backgrounds, homes both broken and together.
They fight hard for us, spilling blood and tears, as they march in adverse weather.

We are a country of heroes, from the war for independence to Memorial Day.
We celebrate our troops with parades and medals for allowing us to stay.
From late-night watches and military drills to short breaks home and moments to reap,
They sacrificed their time with loved ones and family so ours we could keep.

We are a country of heroes, who honor our veterans and actives for a few hours
But then leave them grossly unemployed and in need of welfare for food to devour.
We are a country of heroes, who act in mob mentality for fear of ground zero.
From barbeques and drinking binges, we begin to forget our once-glorified heroes.

We are a country of heroes, and no, I am not in a single branch of the military,
But I have friends and family who have served overseas; both are dear to me.
If we are a country of heroes, then show respect and long-lasting love to their service
Because they throw so much away for us, and honestly, we don't deserve them.

*Less than 1 percent of American citizens serve in the military; although you may not support the war, support that brave warrior.

Love as a Commodity

In this Common Era we as a generation live in a capitalist society,
One that promotes self-indulgence and extreme value in commodity.
We are taught to place value on trivial and material things.
Let love's worth become measured, not in vows but in the price of the weddings.

Young minds quickly learn the lesson that teaches self-gratification.
They sell their souls in favor of the rewards from this new infatuation
Because love is no longer about what you can do together while enamored;
It's becoming intoxicated on what others can do for them, hammered.

Love has become tragically commercialized, sold in stores, corners, and online.
It is cheapened, bought, sold, exchanged, and lacks originality through pick-up line.
Women may argue that they need security not finance or new Prada bags,
Both carelessly carry their anger and past resentment in emotional bags.

Men idolize athletes, celebrities, and musicians for the availability of women,
So focus on gaining mass amounts of riches, queens becomes bitches for men.
People living in low-income houses sport dub rims and the latest Jordan's.
Though calm in public, they're restless over poverty caused from the aforementioned.

With divorce rates shooting up and then stabilizing at a 50 percent ratio,
It's obvious that what the world needs is love but has made it the first thing to go.
The Cost of Love is a lesson in this, for love should be priceless.
Don't let modern trend dictate its value, as its truth is timeless.

Mother's Hands and Father's Words

I am the child of two great people, who laid the foundation for my life,
Implanting valuable lessons of both love and hate to handle times of strife.
I have no memories of them together only of them apart,
But from this foundation, they bore the creation of this fragile and flexible heart.

Mother's hands were kind and soft, well aged and bathed with experience.
Teachings of cultural recipes were written down and filled stomachs' contents.
Mother's hands were brutal yet loving, both chastising me with belts and cords.
Mother's hands reached out and bought games that we couldn't afford.

Father's words bore great strength and taught self-respect and consistency of task.
They gave opinions of both honesty and courage without a prerequisite that I ask.
Father's words bombarded me like bombs when it came to disclosing my identity,
And I began to feel troubled by feelings of inferiority over my own masculinity.

Mother's words echoed in churches and were bathed in different linguistics,
Churches that led to both increased in intergroup love and hate, sociological statistics.
Mother's words grew silent when on hot-topic issues I would lament.
Mother's words were loving and firm, a good foundation of cement.

Father's hands were rough with experience of both building and dismantling things.
He taught me about cars, women, construction, and the weight of engagement rings.
Hands that both gave and taught me firm handshakes on days of graduation,
Hands that poured congratulatory shots that led to generational inebriation.

My heart was built on unstable ground that solidified under times of great stress.
By mother's and father's words that would give strangers and enemies, "God bless."
My heart has been both shattered and discarded by those whom I cared for.
Life's lesson has taught me that no one will hurt me or love me more
Than my mom or dad; I can't change them, but I smile, as I am glad.

What It Means to Be (a Victim)

What it means to be a victim is to lose your sense of identity,
All those things that made you "You" are taken away unjustly.
Your name, which you are given and held so much worth,
Becomes ignored and forgotten like an unattended birth.

What it means to be a victim is to lose the clothes you wear,
To have all the things that you valued striped away without a care.
What it means to be a victim is to know that an important part of you is broken
Because sometimes a stranger or a familiar had plundered all you were, stolen.

What it means to be a victim is to lose your voice,
Knowing that all of you was lost at someone else's choice.
Sadly what it means to define someone as a victim
Is that only one out of seven of their peers will listen.

*Fifty-four percent of sexual assaults are never reported, with two-thirds of them from people we know.

Invincible

Many people have wondered when we learned we weren't invincible.
Did we learn of the deficits in our invincibility when we were three?
When mother and father's divorce and fighting were over me?

When children heard their first curse word
Instead of playful rhymes from Big Bird.
Was invincibility lost in the eyes of a child
When he saw advertisements of *Girls Gone Wild?*

Did we learn to lose and let go of our invincibility in favor of sexual casualties?
Only to let words like *polygamy* and *sodomy* lead to fear of diseases, HIV.
Was it the deceiving smiles of loved ones that led to infections, not one but three.

When did mother learn that for what her child yearned she could not accept?
So instead saw strange love mentioned in the tale of Sodom and Gomorra a threat.
Is invincibility lost not in the shadow of the dark but in the absence of one little spark?

When did father carry the burden that his arms were becoming weak, not stronger?
He pushed his anger, masculinity, and virtue, causing detachment to last longer.
Was invincibility forsaken over the only truth in American equality was
That lives no matter what size could be ended by gunshot ruckus?

Life's Anthem

Life and light fill my eyes as I stare momentarily at the sunrise.
A smile appears to me most dear, ignorant of yesterday's or today's fear.
And in my first steps off my bed, cheerful images fill my head.

We are feet that move forward in charge of our destiny.
Where others were robbed of these chances and opportunity.

I look at the world while inhaling fresh breath into my system,
Unsure if the day laid out for me will make me its victim.
I am happy and grateful for all things in front of me, be they man made or by divinity.

We are hands that smack, push, and prepare to grab,
That rise in self-defense as some are shot or stabbed.

I am relieved yet stressed over college tuition, career goals, and personal fruition.
I am a son of a mother and a father who saw my educational future, a premonition.
These are words bound to paper that I write; MLA betrayed me and forgot to cite.

We are more than Facebook pictures and statuses.
We are overworked and underpaid students preparing for classes.
Yes this is Finals Week, so you may see lots of *FML,**
But we are young and have life; don't forget to *LOL.***

*FML (Fuck my life)
**LOL (Laugh out loud)

Coercive Indian Education

Native-born children learned wise ways before exposure to ideas of pilgrims,
Knowledge given from nurturing and loving mothers and fathers, from elders.
Knowledge was passed down like nourishment from mother to child eagle,
Feeding hungry minds, making them spiritually wealthy like kings, regal.
Family ties were strong and tribal languages spoken, colored with culture in the open.

Then the whites came under an assumed decree of divinity,
Taking homeland under the gaze of manifest destiny.
Forced onto land that was not of our forbearers and suffering cultural degradation.
Children were kidnapped from home and subjected to Anglo-prescribed humiliation,
Denied access to words of comfort in language, held in boarding schools like forts.

In modern times, elders look back and remember in frustration
And can remember government attempts at tribal assimilation.
In their own words, they were a "Lost and stolen generation."
You can be a reservation born, suffer from educational and socioeconomic disparity.
You can be an urban born, a mestizo like me, torn in two and exposed to poverty.

(In spite of the image of the rich Indian, due to Indian-gaming profits, a majority of First
Nations people live below the poverty line. This is due to high unemployment, ranging
between 60 and 80 percent, and inadequate housing.)

Unwanted Legacy

She looked so good you just couldn't let her go
Even though she pleaded desperately, screaming, *No.*

You tried to calm her down by kissing her neck;
All she knew was being there was her regret.

You walked away at the completion of your deed
Not knowing the child you left behind, your seed.

The Boy Who Chased the Sparrows

The boy who chased the sparrows
Ran swiftly through the autumn winds,
Trying to run from summer's end;
Arms reluctantly embracing today,
A sad tear drops as the sparrows fly away.

Home

Walking back from church to a gray car
Painted black with bruises and a new scar.
A child unaccepted lay broken in mother's arms,
A child rushed to ICU, sounds of ambulance alarms.

He tried to lay his head in green pastures to which his Sheppard had led him.
Ever so hopeful for acceptance, he was unaware the pastor's sons dreaded him.

Staying hidden with imaginary friends in the library
Because the boys outside wanted to inflict injury.
A stranger to the playground, he hesitated,
Knowing unkind faces and words waited.

And when that boy had been painted blue,
His brother knew not what he could do
Except finish him up; he was through.

A home is not a place where we lay our head.
A home is a place we no longer feel dead.
Both vivid and full of hope,
Any injury sustained we could cope.

My home lay in the arms of whoever could have me,
Even if it meant being loved momentarily.
So now the child lives lost within this disparity
While he remembers those who mocked in hilarity.

Stereotypes

You want to see a Black stereotype, go to a Black ghetto.
There you'll see boys trying to prove their manhood like Pinocchio.
You want to see a Chinese stereotype, go to little Chinatown.
Hear thick accents and eyes that squint, smile, or frown.

You want to see a gay stereotype, go to San Francisco Pride parade.
Witness both lisp and bent wrist of gay men trying to get laid.
You want to see a Muslim stereotype, go to a mosque.
Watch them bow in humility and modesty but still get carded at airport kiosk.

If you want to disprove these ignorant images of grand community,
Go out to these places and talk to them, and see what builds this diverse unity.
See that religion, sex, and race encompass a variety of creeds
That, by stereotyping, you inflict upon them great misdeeds.

The Levee

Tucked between the long, stretching veins of South Stockton's 8th and Houston,
Lays a sleeping, monstrous river nestled between two shores of hand-packed earth.
Though man made in its origin, it is nature's touch that nurtures it;
Nature's warm clay acts as an incubator, giving life to its hidden children,
With little creatures like rabbits, snakes, lizards, and squirrels pulled from its womb.

Trees scarred with lovers' names etched onto its skin,
Incapable of hearing its screams over the sound of their hearts' enamored rhythm.
The ground is sprinkled with cookie-cutter-shaped rocks and old bike trails,
Of uneven ground, fire pits, and earth mounds all decorating this natural playground.

The levee sings the triumphant songs of boys riding free to new, unknown thrills,
Plays melodies through the whispering trees of lovers' oaths made whole on its hills.
The levee remains a place to me that is more than its beauty and potency in reverie,
But a place in present existence, in which there is possibility to create a new memory.

Follow Me (Social Networks)

Follow me, find me, friend me, and like my status or LMS.
Are all attention-seeking behaviors leaving me with their friendships to dismiss?
When youths of young virtue who lack connections to culture, community, and family
Try finding that feeling of filling on the Internet, it can spell disaster for them instantly.

When you are only hot if you are the current trending topic,
So they devalue and sell themselves just to stay on top of it.
Not knowing how much of their personal rights and privacy
Are being sold to corporate executives and online dangers so cheaply.

Now the Internet is not to blame as it is just a tool, from which much can be obtained.
When parents can't teach their kids, and peers are left responsible, it is maintained.
Does the Like button represent nourishment in the form of attention unconditionally?
When you pour so much out there for all to see, your addiction is fed momentarily.

Runaway Bullet

A parenting gun lets loose its wild and loud child into the crowded streets.
A sound banging louder than amplified car stereos filled with music beats.
It travels silently through the shadows of a few different alleyways,
Piercing through government houses and striking children in the hallways.

There is no need of a parent gun that shot the bullet that found home happily
But a great need for the parent that left the shooter on his own when he was three.
Inner-city violence makes sad music that outweighs concert violins,
So, fathers, stick around; teach your boys how to become men.

Us versus Them

Look at them; look at all of them, these disgusting people.
They steal our jobs, money, land, and our country's resources!
We are the ones who belong in this land, gave to it, and developed it into our home.
It should not be corrupted by those who forsook theirs and should be left alone!

Look at them; look at all of them, these idiotic and incompetent people.
They are unable to do well in school and tag up our streets and cities!
We are the ones who first laid ground here and built beautiful neighborhoods;
But they fill it with trash-like people and tarnish them, turning them into 'hoods.

Look at them; look at all of these unwanted and ignorant people.
They speak a tongue that is not ours and butcher our language!
We are the ones who write the laws, teach the classes, and control the media;
They complain and say that they don't understand and ask for interpreters.

Look at them; look at all of them, these humble and discriminated-against people.
Right now they appear easily recognizable and brown in coloration.
But we were once them: we are Irish, Catholic, African and are now Americans.
So remember all of this as we are foreigners to the Native Americans.

Modern Day Warriors (Gangs)

Brown, black, yellow, and red children run wildly throughout the streets
Like Aztec, Zulu, Boxers, and Apache warriors fighting European fleets.
They arm themselves with guns in the place of spears, arrows, tomahawks, and fists,
Gunning down rivals and innocent civilians, putting names on tombstones like hit lists.

Gang members cling to fundamental countercultural ideals, creating an infrastructure.
Gangs act like families defending, supporting, killing, and fending for one another.
Children whose moms work two jobs, who lack parents that are willing to parent,
Hustle hard for drug money in order to keep the lights on and pay their rent.

The warrior code is one that requires strict ritualistic initiation
While brothers, *hermanos*,* and cousins get jumped on in isolation.
They decorate their bodies with tattoos and colors, learning which to hate,
Fifteen-year-old fingers are ready to assassinate without need to hesitate.

When a brother, a homie, or a cuz that shared time, money, and parties is killed,
He becomes venerated as the streets run red with opposing blood being spilled.
These modern day warriors protect their *barrios*, homes, and neighborhoods
While they run their base of operations on land where a playground once stood.

When one of them distinguishes themselves with academic achievement,
They must get jumped out by them as heads smash against the pavement.
Concrete foundations serve as cold-stone reminders of where it is safe for them to be.
The holistic beauty of the city is divided by fear of entering enemy-gang territory.

Brown, black, yellow, and red children have their hands stained with gunpowder,
Are all buried indiscriminately in adjacent grave plots with a funeral flower.
They arm themselves with guns, fellowship, and drugs but not with knowledge.
They continue to repeat this cycle that keeps these ethnic kids out of college.

Hermanos is Spanish for *brothers*.

Their Eyes are on the Door (The Gay Scene)

Their eyes were on the door of clubs like Casablanca, where they wait to judge.
They clutter together like leaves stuck in a drain, old ways refusing to budge.
Their eyes are always on the door, waiting for the appearance of a new face,
For which to satisfy their thirstiness, doing anything for the pleasure of a taste.

Their eyes are always on the door, perpetuating acts that let HIV flourish.
Where young hearts seeking older ones become objectified, no need to nourish.
Older hearts, poisoned from their arrival on the scene and past misuse,
Seek to rejuvenate them by dating younger men and only manage to inflict abuse.

Their eyes are always on the door, waiting on a new face to appear,
One who is unfamiliar to all the people whose name they could truthfully smear.
They are quick to spit game in an attempt to ascertain this new unknown name,
Becoming spiteful over swallowing their rejection, like an erection without a name.

Their eyes are always on the door, for fear of a stranger's unwelcome assault
But spread hateful messages and gay bash themselves, banging heads on asphalt.
They fuck raw, "Hell it's only once; I can risk it,"
And ignore that it only takes once to be a statistic.

Their eyes are always on the door, waiting for the assembly of attractive features,
Priding themselves on facades and reinforcing them with photoshopped pictures.
They perpetuate views of themselves and idolize divas that appear to be on top,
Only to reveal who they are behind closed doors with questions of, "Bottom or top?"

Their eyes are always on the door, lacking much depth the shallow at the party.
As they remain thirsty and unhappy, only finding relief in their bottle of Blue Bacardi.
They are quick to frustrate, intoxicate, and celebrate but not to unify against Prop 8.
They lay happily unaware and confused as to their immoral acts, self-defecate.

El Único Deseo de una Mujer con Embargo*

She is riddled with anxiety and allows for her tongue to tie itself
As dreams and possibilities are hidden away from others on the shelf.
Her heart is filled heavy with terror and *miedo*,* only sweetened by Latin flavor
As she struggles hard to keep everything organized with her one-woman labor.

She wishes so deeply to be appreciated without need of a question;
However, their eyes gaze at TV screens, unaware of her storm within.

She stops herself from speaking words and discussions that are argumentative.
She tells herself, "It won't change anything," and these thoughts become repetitive.
Her back is tired from helping out the hospitalized elderly;
Her soul is tired from working hard to escape poverty.

She wishes selfishly to say these words she holds back with hesitation,
Only to choke as she holds them back, unable to breathe without ventilation.

She wishes that they would do more to enrich themselves and the apartment,
But very little is done, and they call themselves supportive by paying the rent.
Her mind wishes so badly to be appreciated and to be able to rely on them.
But without her words being spoke, they continue not knowing her storm within.

El Único Deseo de una Mujer Con Embargo is Spanish for *The Only Wish of a Woman with Doubt*
Miedo is Spanish for *fear*.

Feathers

If I had to be an inanimate object, I would be a solitary feather.
I can fly on my own or travel great distances once bounded together.
When an individual feather is set out into the world on its air currents,
It can be forever suspended or become pushed and trapped in a sense.

Feathers capable of levitating on their own, once unified, create improvement
Like those who strive together creating Black-, Brown-, or Red-Power movement.
With feathers united together under the brilliance of a wing called Community,
We lose the name the United States of America in favor of a simple name, Unity.

But alas, hatred has clipped our wings, so here comes increased tension and terror.
We foolishly attribute momentary acts to permanent Ultimate Attribution Error.*
I am a student of Gordon Allport, who wants to find *The Nature of Prejudice*,
So maybe then we can find equality and justice, not caring only about "Just us."

*Pettigrew, 1979, Theory of Ultimate Attribution Error.

Peacock

They throw on colorful shoes with matching fitted hats,
Glorify a lifestyle they never lived with recognized gang tats.
They put time into constructing an image that they can sell,
Not knowing that they can only succeed at being themselves.

They live transparent yet color-coordinated lives,
All smoke-and-mirror attempts leading to compromise.

They throw on colorful shoes with matching fitted hats,
Embrace the negative images associated with prison tats.
They put time into constructing an image that they can sell,
Losing themselves in favor of living a fiction's fairy tale.

Deprivation

Let me take a moment to talk to the adults,
To help them recognize their parenting faults.
I come with this spoken truth and simple warning
That desire is passed down, so you determine childish wanting.

Mothers and fathers who were robbed of education in order to pursue work
Often form that first foundation that emphasizes the importance of homework.
They see the world that is made accessible through academic advancement.
They sacrifice themselves so that their children can obtain educational achievement.

Mothers and fathers who lacked the toys that were important to them in childhood
Will continue to endorse concepts of materialism that perpetuate fabulous 'hoods.
They see the world measured only in material made easy with Black Friday sales.
Parents lose the value of Thanksgiving by ignoring family-appreciation tales.

A Woman Called America

North America was a Native American woman with many children.
She offered kindness and warmth to European men in need.
They abused her and pimped her out, calling her "Squaw!"*
They made her a banner and a dress for her to wear.

They promised equality with their invention of democracy,
Yet her first children were unrecognized until the 1920s.
This dress was red, the color of her children's blood.
This dress was white, after those who shed their blood.
This dress was blue, after the tears her children cried.

They honored her with a shawl with stars,
Stars that looked down at forced marches.
They embroidered an eagle onto this once-proud woman.
They named her America, although that was not her name.

They created Dawes roles, which registered and took Indian land.
They carved monuments into her body as testimony to their existence.
Her children's tongues lost their ability to speak what she had taught them.
This all became easier when they were drunk off of foreign rum.
Here stands America draped in a name and dress that were not her own.

Squaw is an English equivalent for *cunt*.

World's Deadliest Black Man

Which is deadlier, a Black man with a loaded gun
Or a Black man seeking education, providing for his son?
Which do we fear, the notion of inner-city aggression
Or the educated and proud who pass on college lessons?

Which is deadlier, a magazine of bullets or a cartridge of pens,
When two-thirds of gun owners suffer deaths at their own weapons?
Which lasts longer, the sound of shots fired at a politician
Or the sound of words that become contagious, fueling revolution?

Which is more salient, thug life or a life of wisdom,
When one murders and the other enriches our brethren?
Which is more broadcasted and spread through the media
Like an infection that disproportionately affects us like chlamydia?

Which is more salient, negative or positive associations
When societal perspectives become promoted by institutions?
Which is the one that you choose to endorse
When I give you reality, and you see metaphors?

Chapter II: Identity in Loss

In times of tragedy or despair, we find ourselves searching through memories, thoughts, and pictures, trying to find out who we were and who we are. It is through loss that we sometimes find out more about ourselves than we had previously been made aware of. We construct ourselves in the eyes of how we believed others had seen us, especially when those others were significant ones that have left us.

The shades that this chapter paints are those of deep-blue hues, colors that pour over these pages like rolling rivers. Tears, much like rivers, can erase testimony to long-standing foundations with time. As these poems are crafted, maybe your blue tears will erode something deeper.

Revenge

I spell *revenge* success; it is the value in the word *bless.*
I am feet moving forward both steady and experienced, obtaining more not less.
As I push myself hard between business meetings as a full-time student,
I have been placed with a great title, not the one you gave like *impudent.*

It is through the pain of heartache, paternal neglect, abandonment, and ignorance
That I put the past and those behind me and wish them luck chasing my footprints.
From me changing the negative association of my name to it having fame.
It is through wisdom passed onto me that I temper actions out of necessity.

A former label of *worthlessness* unknowingly placed upon me
Appears now as a fallacy spoken by those filled with jealousy.
People see now how I stand in this fleeting but glorious moment
But are all unaware of the more than seven times I fell, falling monument.

I write this simple and just ode
Living by the proverb, "Revenge is a dish best served cold."
May every degree be a triumphant and well-deserved decree
That you aren't the one in charge of my life; I've given the reigns to me.

I spell *revenge* success; it's settling for more not less.
I am full-time student, part-time worker, and proudly a published author,
Which means I'm not struggling with essays while you were doing different *eses.**
Now quiet down into silence and see what I've obtained in your absence.

*Eses is Spanish slang for *men.*

59+

I am a man who has learned that love exists in neither form of man nor woman.
Now the first lesson on conditional love may sound similar to daddy issues,
But it was he who gave me feelings of worthlessness momentarily quieted by tissues.

I have tried earning the romantic favors of fifty-nine men and women, respectively.
Each case has led me to contemplate and temper my next assailant carefully.
My heart lay at times in small pieces, both scattered and broken,
Yet due to this shattering, I have been able to give the world a poetic token.

So when new eyes, which lay future promises of positive fruition or negative demise,
Tell me that they love me wholly without more than a month of knowing me,
So it is with due cause I cannot rest assured that these sweet nothings are not lies.
As time and time again, people have sown in seeds of love and broken these ties.

I have made my peace with much of this though my heart is now bottomless.
Listen carefully, for therein lies at the bottom of a heart-shaped well
A man who silently weeps for fifty-nine times he has fell.

Death of a Nice Guy

Giving great gifts of feeling and romance make me wonder,
Was attempting to be nice to you a good thing or a blunder?
I deliver both kind and sweet words through text and phone calls;
You get distracted hanging on the tip of someone else's balls.

When you know that someone is feeling you and will stay by your side,
Those mutual emotions that you showed with pride you now selfishly hide.
Being kind to so many women and men has left me with deep-seated inadequacies.
When I'm being honest to you about where I stand, and they feed me fallacies.

Women complain and grow upset, spitting poison, calling men dogs,
But isn't a bitch a dog of a different gender, growing bitter of past handlers?
Don't complain about not having someone who will support you and do you right
When your real interest is with that guy who left you hanging solo the other night.

So to the men and women who are reading this note or blog,
Clear your mind up, stop living in uncertainty: fog.
Because you know damn well you don't want a nice guy like me;
All I can do is wish you well and that you reap what you sow happily.

Distance

I cannot shrink the distance between two people, no matter how strong I become.
Although nearsighted eyes did see this as a possibility, this is what I must overcome.
The distance between us cannot be easily filled by sweet words and gestures.
So I ask, "Is it wrong to believe in us and that this distance could conquered?"

Though you do care for me and me for you,
I spend time quietly, unsure what to do,
What to say, how to feel;
More importantly, how to heal?

Clever and sweet words both slid and flew off your tongue,
I hoped that your good-bye was not something I had to overcome.
I am filled with doubt, regret, and happiness,
And though I cry, it is under no new duress.

With these hands I would like to shorten that distance from you to me.
I wish to naively believe in this possibility that it may come easily.
It was not wrong to try, and I did enjoy trying.
Nor is it wrong to cry, so I will enjoy crying.

I cannot ask you to "Be My Last"* or expect to distract you from living your life.
I held on to so many empty nothings and hoped that I would be kept in your life.
Yes our paths will cross again as you had just said,
But I can't help but cling to these images of you in my head.

There lies a bottle of Patron, a copy of the Bible leading me to my father's throne.
I wish to temper my actions with inebriation, to be left to myself, alone.
The distance between two people can be shortened with communication,
But due to this lack of reciprocity, I fear of calling you due to hesitation.

*"Be My Last" is a song by Japanese-American recording artist Utada Hikaru.

Death of a Lion

I look at angels and demons and have lost my ability to distinguish
Between them; as I look at old and fond memories, I'm filled with anguish
As they both hide their identity behind pure and similar smiles.
It gave me purpose to contemplate trusting you for a while.

New facts arise, and my anger erodes at my heart as if to smite me.
Leaving a coal-like blackness, a poisonous gift called envy.
You danced around the heads of other male members, polygamy.

I am anger laced with sadness, poisoned by love.
Emotions, which were like strong tides with a Leo,
Like a star secretly manipulating my ebb and flow.

Blinding me to obvious labels placed on you: hoe.
Named after a lion, I should have known you were lying
About the other guys with whom you were lying.

I am feet that move forward,
And though I refuse to face you, I'm no coward.
As eyes that were once closed now open see you,
And both angels and demons teach me how to perceive you.

Prisoner

Emotions become prisoners as they condensate into tears
Held behind thick black eyelashes like prison bars.
Memories of lovers of the Latin persuasion not lost
But held onto regardless of emotional and mental health cost.

Eyes that stare at its prisoners as though a warden,
Wait solely for love's growth in a human flower garden.
Though I stand with my captives, I too am a prisoner of love.
For I stand lonely in my guard tower, captive to ideas of past love.

Prison Rose

The light that breaks through the night sky
And gives birth to dawn awakens me.
Sitting on the rooftop watching the world
Asleep and watching yesterday's end.
The rose that grew just outside my window
Rests with you, tenderly held to your breast.

Trapped in these melancholy walls,
You, the fragrance from the rose, grace my cheek
And makes this place feel like home.
That "home" lies in your arms gently pressed
Against your heart; it will shelter you if you let it.

The moments pass into hours; these tears fade to sighs.
The clustering hopes of this town forge this single
Thought, delicately unraveled in your hands.
My heart captured in a glance, a secondary romance,
These words tied tightly to those lips are now freed.

Cold Kisses and Even Colder Words

These simple days that pass by sadly like the tears that roll down my cheek.
Another wasted Saturday has rolled by, and I cannot help but taste bitterness.
I am sitting in this room of mine; I will soon have to leave.
The promise of tomorrow seems to be one that cannot be fulfilled.

These days when we don't meet, and all we can offer each other are cold words.
If I could be cradled for a while, I would love for you to be the one to cradle me.
I let you, another person I reach out to that was so distant, touch me so tenderly.
These words mean nothing to someone who never was close to me except in reverie.

Even in my dreams, all I can do is watch you walking a different path that I can't reach.
All I can do is cradle myself and let these moments pass by.
Why am I still waiting for someone that can't hold on, see, or hear me?

Will I ever be just good enough; at times when I look into the mirror, I see nothing.
Yet is it bad to look into it every day, hoping to see something new?
This bitter poison is one that I have grown familiar with, but it has lost its potency.

Jesus

While softly being embraced by the skies,
I closed these eyes, which were blind to love
And found myself free-falling into your arms.
As ephemeral dreams transitioned into joyful dreams,
I stood up as you embraced my sins.

I walk forward in a time that knows neither I nor
Your name or presence but lives lavishly in your absence.
I open my eyes that caught glimpse of that,
And walked toward a time in which you exist.

My arms spread wide trying to let go of my sins and embrace yours.
Wings, which were not strong enough to hold you up,
Have gradually disappeared into that place called the past.
Your voice quietly disappeared as my eyes shut.

I walked by your side as your shadow evaporated in front of me.
While still embracing my sins and learning yours, we created new ones.
While being cradled in the warm embrace of Mother Nature's clay,
I awoke from sorrowful dreams to see you gone.

Jobs (a Metaphor for Dating)

I put on my best suits and airs wishing to show you that I am the best dressed.
I tried on different styles of clothes, and at our first interview you were impressed.
I spent time on grooming, hoping to have a place to stay, not to get in between.
I waited patiently for a phone call of the position that you enjoyed this prestige.

When I got the notification that I had piqued your interest, you made me a new hire.
I thought I was the only one for you, so all previous employees you'd fire.
I grew heated and somewhat hot for you, this feeling called passion.
I was indulging myself in your presence, my romantic-love ration.

Then came the time when we had both gotten comfortable within the month I was here.
Your mind had seen me simply as a part timer, but I saw you as my future career.
So it was at that time I decided to put in my formal two weeks' notice.
At the sight of my attitude, you decided it was for the best to protest this.

I learned only then when my paystub came in would you lay with me
As I was your part-time lover, and you had a full-time husband, a hidden faculty.
I had always wondered why this job came with no medical or other benefits.
In this moment of hindsight in which I had blindness,
I became aware of my title of friends with benefits.

Dolor (La Significa de tu Nombre)

Los dolores que compartimos juntos
Ahorita nos dejan solos y separados.
Yo quiero decirte "Te amo," pero el tiempo,
El tiempo hace las palabras desaparecer

Estoy desesperado para decirte esas palabras,

Esas palabras que te dije el último día que te toqué, el último día que te besé.
Dolor es una palabra que no puedo pronunciar, el sentimiento que no me deja solo
Alegría, su hermana, es una amiga que no conozco, como su cara hermosa

Quizás es posible obtener una historia nueva
Pero el miedo saca mi coraje y lo quebranta!
En el espacio que me dejaste, yo digo "Te amo."
Aunque estoy sincero, no vas a regresar.

Estoy desesperado para decirte esas palabras,
Esas palabras que te dije el último día que te toqué, el último día que te besé.
Dolor es una palabra que no puedo pronunciar, el sentimiento que no me deja solo
Alegría, su hermana, es una amiga que no conozco, como su cara hermosa

Quizás es posible para obtener una historia nueva,
Pero miedo saca mi coraje y romperlo.
En el espacio que me dejaste, yo digo "Te amo."
Aunque soy sincero, no vas a regresar.

Letter to Arvin

Today I wrote a letter that I probably will not send.
It described the broken heart we both feel and my intent to mend.
You introduced me to the song "Firework," by Katy Perry two years ago,
So maybe it was significant that on the Fourth of July to your house I did go.

You were 326 miles away from me for two years prior.
It shrunk down to a twenty-minute drive to you, my past desire.
Here we were for the first time, and you stood at five foot nine.
Sudden burst of nostalgia erupted within me, past thoughts of when you were mine.
I stood outside with you after helping you get a friend home before it was too late,
Conversed with you in your car, making you laugh and watching your face illuminate.

I told you in the letter I dared not send just how much to me you meant.
You were the sweet voice on the phone and the warmth on top of cold cement.
Like the fireworks, I held you high in the air, waiting for you to burst; explosive.
However since then, the sadness that haunts me is eating away at my heart; corrosive.
I sincerely hoped that not one single letter of the words I wrote would hurt you.
The sole hope was that it could indicate that this situation you could get through.

I told you never to lose your smile, *"Mi sonrisa,"** as you're the reason behind mine.
I hoped foolishly that this unsent letter would help reassure you, "That it will be fine."
I know how much J. P. and the many others have hurt you,
But if you need a rope to pull through with, I'm here for you.

**Mi sonrisa* is Spanish for *my smile.*

Nostalgia

A friend called Nostalgia crept into my bed,
Painting vivid galleries of past memories in my head.
I used to say, "I would trade a minute of the past for an hour in the future,"
So my fingertips wait patiently for a time machine and its dials to configure.

Heavy eyes flutter recklessly, trying to avert themselves from the present
While coffee-brown eyes pour warmly over past letters in the present.
The hourglass tips over and spills its sands upon two hands that cannot catch it
But continue ticking uninterrupted as they whine to count time at my resentment.

My grandfather clock comforts me with its long, deep, and heavy rings.
Tear-soaked hands moistened in their attempt to comfort are incapable of embracing.
A smile appears both brief as I scoop up the remaining sands,
And my heart beats rhythmically with those two counting hands.

A friend called Nostalgia crept into my bed,
Shared generously moments of happiness and those of dread.
I would trade an hour of the future for a minute of the past,
But I am not foolish enough to make my home in the past.

Heart on a Sleeve

I used to wear my heart on my sleeve,
Showing you what you wanted so you wouldn't leave.
So when you departed, fleeting feelings of being broken hearted.
I decided to place it in my pocket, held safe; no need to lock it.

I met many a gold digger, who in wealth did seek me,
But the only gold they found was my heart not tainted by envy.
Meeting people who promised to make it rain expected Indian dances.
Using monetary value to hide pain and a poor attempt to capture glances.

My heart is a collage of sweet and bitter moments, of love lost and found,
Of divine, sweeping moments and of those making tears fall: earthbound.
It is a picture on display not for a select few, but proudly visible for all to view.
I would never trade it in for something else, and it wasn't something you knew.

Lost in Love

In the time it takes for a heart to skip a beat, in the time it takes for a tear to fall,
I will have fallen for you; the exact reason why I cannot recall.
Although as of late we have been plagued with dead-air phone calls,
You should know the reason I trip is because for you I fall.

I am lost in love but not in its embraces.
For love is a wanderer with many changing faces.
I who have lost something so important over something so small,
Now wait idly by for us to fill this dead-air phone call.

Angels Crying (In A minor)

The words you spoke that night taught me loneliness.
Eyelashes flap across that wide space called time.
Staring deeply into that lost place of preserved memories called the past,
A heartache appears both brief and sweet, and I honor it with a tear.

We choked at feelings we didn't know we had, something called fear.
Hands grew anxious yet desired the company of each other.
If you were my obsession, then loving you was my compulsion.
This is my disorder, and no it isn't generalized anxiety; it's the story of you and me.

Knowing love is knowing God, so I knew it was not wrong to try and make it.
When we knew we were clumsy enough to fall in love, that we could break it.
Hearts were pure, filled with tender emotion, and I knew we both felt alone.
I hoped that we could be alone together; for past grievances we could atone.

A cold glass that once held the contents of that inebriating liquid called love
That appeared pure and white, a divine symbol like that of Moses's dove,
Has showed me its cold glimmer, and I know it is not wrong to love.
I can neither ask you to come back nor move forward, but I know you will.

My charcoal-black eyes were filled with joy over your missed phone calls, my thrill.
I once loved without fear, and I let you see my scars and bruises,
Some self-inflicted and others through neglect and past misuses.
My love was that of a charity, giving away freely to those in need.

Your love was like a job, only employing those who fed on greed.
Eyes flutter in a dim-lit room void of both your presence and ours.
As moments turn to minutes, which spill emptily into hours;
These are the sounds of angels crying in A minor.

El Rio y El Rey

Your name is Juan Ríos,
Y estoy enamorado con tus labios.
Es poesía por ti mi alegría,
Es una manera para decirte "Buenas Días."

Eres mi querido amigo,
Y me encanta pasar tiempo contigo.
Yo quiero nadar en tus ríos secretos,
Y hacer tus labios míos.

Me llamo El Rey y me llamas Reymundo,
Por un mes estaba parte de tu mundo.
Yo soy tu amigo y no quiero más,
Pero caminar a tu lado en vez de atrás.

Pinocchio

I stare at you and sing high and low notes for you, waiting for a simple call,
And I know that you are waiting for someone else's love and to fall.
My tears become orphans that fall down like false memories of love that did not exist
And evaporate, forming a melancholy lingering mist.

I know that you are being pulled on your strings by Gepetto,
He who questions and validates your manhood, dear Pinocchio.

I wait for you to stop being Pinocchio; I wait for you to show
Me that you are a real boy, not some silent toy.
Feelings for you are unrequited and unneeded,
But I still give to you until my love is depleted.

I know that I can't compete with her and lay defeated.
She is your blue fairy who you may one day marry.

I am the wish of happiness that disappears when the lights dim,
And I am aware that my limitation is that I am not a woman.
I am not jealous as my heart is no home for that green-eyed monster;
I just wish you'd turn and see that my heart is fertile land for you to conquer.

Your Receiver is Broken

You poured your love out like a river into unknown sources.
You drew it deep from a well, love's natural resources.
But your receiver is broken, and you craved for love open,
Honest, and unconditional, but you've been conditioned not to receive.

You have been unjustly deceived by both familiar and strange faces.
They left your heart in all these strange and wrong places.
You kept your legs closed and your heart open,
But this safety measure left your receiver broken.

You poured out love from a well that had seemingly gone dry,
Lost the ability to read someone's attention from their eye.
You transmit love across a wire, hoping to be someone's desire,
But your receiver is broken, and you've left your legs open.

The Well is Dry

I poured my wavering emotions that I was not strong enough to overcome
Into that dry well of inspiration, called poetry, until it overflowed.
The water surged into the well with such great force and turbidity
That tears flowed out of the cracks in its walls,
Which had once been bonded as tightly as we were.

The sound of the cracking well is music most powerful if only for its pain,
For which it invokes, for which it was forged from, for which we gave it.
The sound of both loving words and those that became *hueco** flutter about.

They become strong like waves from that sea of despair fueled by Weeping Moon.
The cliffs of my heart that we built together have been eroded and broken down.

These rocks both strong and sturdy were once pieces of my heart turned cold and hard.
These rocks that glimmer like diamonds when bathed in the well's miserable waters.
I hold one up and whisper into the well, and yet not even my Echo responds to me.
I hold the stone tightly to my breast, warming it with the leftover love my mom gave.
It briefly responds, and I build around this well, which had taken my tears and pain.

I am unsure if I've built a shrine or a mausoleum for my love of you and build on.
Yesterday's condensation of tears turns into today's hard-work sweat.

I build upon this foundation, and in it I find the strength to write you that,
"I am doing fine," as the well hides my voice, and my tears I have learned to rebuild.
Still I leave my lonely hand drifting playfully in the wind for you to take a hold of.

*Hueco is Spanish for *hollow*.

Maple Story

The maple leaves fluttering on the autumn wind,
The shifting colors of the midday sun reflected in the pools below.
I can barely see them now; these are moments lost in the annals of time.
These vibrant colors of autumn vanish into mist before half-open eyes.

With them those long drawn-out days of a time we can't return to.
That promise that you made then, does it still ring true?
The autumn sun's rays break through the maple leaves.
"I believe your promise is too hard for you to keep."

The frigid autumn winds blow gently through this town.
The dancing maple leaves scatter as I walk the path to our old hangout.
A sense of nostalgia sparked by the remnants of your scent carried on the breeze.
I can still hear your words, as fingertips grace our names carved into the wood.

"Even if my promise is too hard to keep, I will give you courage.
Rest assured I will always be there; forever I will be thinking of you."
Even if I can't see you now or feel your hands holding mine,
I can have faith in the promise you entrusted in me, this love.

I can still feel your heart beating with mine.
Even if I can't read those lips that spoke those words.
Even now your words remind me and continue to remain true.
I believe your promise that blooms like a flower in my heart.

The maple leaves flutter on the autumn wind momentarily
As the wind scatters them at my feet, which move forward.
I turn to that place that is held safely within the annals of time
And let the colors of the autumn winds erase this mist.

*Sakura**

The flower petals we cherished wither away;
Yet another year has escaped the both of us.
I hold tightly onto that last petal from our younger days,
But I cannot help but feel regret
For not telling you how I felt then.

The blossoms, those were so beautiful,
Have all but gone now just like you.
As I try tracing my old steps along the road we used to walk,
I pretend to hold your hand just once more
Even though all I have is this last petal.

I can remember the first day of high school,
And how you held onto me so tightly that day.
I can still hear the sound of the girls laughing.
As I chased after my friends, how odd I had looked then.
When I turn the corner and reach them, I awaken into the present…

The cherry blossom is overrated,
Yet it sums up everything we had then:
How something so beautiful fades.
I can still feel your presence as I sit down on the
Bench we used to sit on, in front of your old house.

I close my eyes just a bit,
And I can hear the sound of your heart beating.
You always had a way of making the flowers last
Past spring, but now I can barely see them.
Just please hold me one last time.
I open my eyes, and just like that,
You're here by my side.
If I had one wish to make
Within these last temporal moments with you
*Onegai tsuyoku dakishimete.***

*Sakura is Japanese for *cherry blossoms.*
**Onegai tsuyoku dakishimete is Japanese for *Please hold me tightly.*

When?

When will, "I'll see you soon"
Become today and not someday?

When will you see that I'm worth something,
Something more than your present vision sees?

When will I decide enough is enough
Because you don't appreciate me?

My Heart Is In ICU.

My heart is in ICU.
Yes, it's all because of you.

Now this may sound absurd,
Given the sweetness of your words
Cannot null this unbearable pain
Nor remedy me of the bitterness of Novocain.

The sweetness of your words
Isn't something many deserve,
But it will not dull my pain
No matter how much morphine.

And so my heart is in ICU.
Just know it's all because of you.

Hana no Yuki*

The petals dancing softly in the summer's wind have all but withered now.
Even in the snow, the most beautiful of all has begun to bloom.
Through the cold, the light that is you guided me to a warmer place
Where the flowers continue to bloom through that same light.

The morning dew that shined that day
Moistened your face as we lay across the fresh snow.
Watching how the sky seems to carry on forever into a universe
Where the flowers that bloomed in winter were just as beautiful as you.

The soft petals still dancing on the icy winds begin to engulf us in their scent.
I can see your life inside the mischievous winds that howl at the top of my window.
As you passionately expressed your love, how wild and out of control it was then.
How the times have shaped it to become as beautiful as the snow-covered flowers.

The flower born of snow is a rare and fragile beauty that carries your light.
Its scent is so faint, yet as you press yourself against me in love's warm embrace,
The flower begins to melt and bring spring again where it can be felt even closer.
Though that flower has withered and it is now gone…just like you.

Hana no yuki is Japanese for *Flower of snow*.

Where Did the Butterflies Go?

When simple words that sparked infatuation
Have died, grown bitter, and faded away,
I ask, "Where did the butterflies go?"
The simple things that made hearts grow.

When love's soft lips that graced her cheek,
When lying in someone's arms made hearts peek,
When all these things have lost their meanings,
She asked, "Where did the butterflies go?"

When Father Time's touch has aged his heart,
And he tries to remember where did he start?
As Mother Nature begins to weep,
All the promises he couldn't keep.
He'd ask himself, "Where did the butterflies go?"

When the feelings that filled them up
Led them to pour more alcohol in their cup.
As time passes, no more romances.
So tired of second chances, they ask,
"Where did the butterflies go?"
Empty hands with nothing left to show.

When love was a thing with wings
That flew from our stomach and made us sing,
And our faces no longer glow,
We ask each other, "Where did our butterflies go?"

Eulogy to the Butterflies

The sound of beating wings has stopped.
The last petal from that rainbow rose has dropped.
A single breeze blows through me and pillages my warmth.
I'm standing on a bridge between two ponds, and I let love knock me down.
Life has taught me lessons that sometimes the ones who let us smile make us frown.

The butterflies' wing beats are declining, and my eyelashes beat with them.
Tears cling on to lashes like raindrops on to rose petals, barely holding to the rim.
My feelings of sadness are wrapped around memories of that simple and limited joy.
They become imprinted on me like that last kiss from the creator of these memories, a
boy.

HIV

Today marks that dreaded day
When a three-letter word took your life away.

The life you lived was fun and cool;
Not wearing a condom, you played the fool.

These silent moments pass idly by;
Too bad you can't see your loved ones cry.

FYI (As the Child Cries) (A. A. R.)

You whisper a lie about the past into a familiar ear,
And I must ask myself again, "Why do I wait here?"
Was I just waiting for just one more night together?
As this child cries, its tears seem to run forever.

Chilling in a room that you have abandoned tonight,
I look out Angelica's window and admire your room.
I cradle myself in my blanket (as this child cries),
And you rush into her arms, yet there your heart dies.

The ever-expanding world within his arms (as the child cries)
Erases and corrodes the memories that had tied us together.
The taste of four morphine pills lingers, and morning alarms
All seemed to blend together as my angel had left me a lone feather.

As the child cries,
And beautiful words only die.
Within the child's eyes,
The man lay broken inside.

Love Was

Love was watching the sunset reflected in your eyes,
Feeling the last piece of Trident gum leave my mouth and enter yours.
Love was waking up to a good-morning text from you.

Love was knowing that I was the last voice you heard before the day's close.
Love was knowing that you inspired such uneven prose.
Love was now lying in someone else's bed.

Love was a gift that you hadn't yet given.
Love was a wish and a dream that you shared with someone else.
Love was the lingering wish of happiness I gave you.

Regret

The taste of your lips is like biting into a crisp apple.
It's sweet but leaves me yearning for so much more.

The remnants of yesterday's deeds are still laid in your eyes,
And I still have no clue of how to love you.

You're like reading a book with empty pages,
An unfinished fairy tale with no happy ending.

Still I look through the pages, becoming excited by the past.
I try rewriting our story, but like us, my pen is dead.

I Am

In the words of Emily Dickinson, "I am nobody."
Yes, I am the famous nobody that everyone speaks of.
You have known me all your life but nothing about me.
However, I know all about you because I was there.

When negligent friends and family spoke spiteful words and said,
"Nobody cares about you," yes, I was there, and indeed I did care.
When the one whom you gave your heart to sent it back labeled *return to sender*
And on love you did surrender, you said, "Nobody loves me," and yes, I do love you.

Through quiet nights alone, only disrupted by sounds of unused ring tones,
In your loneliness you cried, "Nobody is here," and indeed, I was there beside you.
When you grew proud of your success with feelings of being blessed,
You said, "Nobody helped me get to where I am," and yes, I was there to help.

In this new moment, you turned into that small mirror known as his eyes,
And as you touch his cheek and ask, "Is anybody there?"
No, anybody was not there; just me, Nobody.
Although I had always stood there, it was for I you did not care.

I Was

I was the wind that kicked at your heels as you walked away.
I was the feeling of an invisible touch caressing your every pore.
I was someone you could never see but you knew was there.
I wished to be held so tightly by you, but like the wind, I fell through your hands.

I was the voice on the other side of the receiver.
I was the smile on your face for one month and eighteen days.
I was the one you called Choco not because I'm dark but because I'm sweet.
I wished to help carry the heavy burden on your shoulders.

I was the anger laced with sadness as you rejected my phone calls.
I was the one who bought you carnations on your birthday.
I was the image over the webcam that stayed up late with you.
I wished for your own happiness but did not know it did not include me.

Empty Eyes

Sitting alone in a room we used to chill in,
The light from the setting sun breaks through the blinds.
Another night I spent being lost in your text message.
Rereading words that sounded so promising,
Those now only serve to cut me so deeply.

Sitting in a dark room where the only light
I can see is the glare from the cell phone screen,
Walking around with a defeated look in my eyes.

The light from the morning sun enters into an empty room
Where I no longer am as I sit on the balcony enjoying the air,
Enjoying the summer hopes that seemed to be captured in a view.
Another day where I'm learning how to laugh without you.

Kiss and Cry

The medicine to heal a broken heart is bitter.
Yet as I trace out time-worn scars with tender hands,
My emotions begin to overflow from the depths of my soul.
If my tears were the rain that fell that evening, then you should know
The image of your face would be reflected in every single drop.

Still, I try to pick up the leftover shards of a broken heart, of our past.
But I still cut myself on every shard while I try to fix it,
Never knowing moving on would be this hard.
When I can't trust even myself, who is there to lean on?

I try to take hold of my wavering emotions, still singing silently to myself,
"We can start over; I need to be with you."
I can still feel my heart racing as I held you close to me; still I wait for your
Phone call, searching through my memories for times when we were happy.
Yet I can't seem to hold on to those.

My wavering emotions I have yet to grab them,
But my hand lingers out for someone else's.
The song of spring lets my heart beat again,
And your cold words have melted into warmth.
Thank you for all of your love.

Requiem

A single silver tear rolls down the side of my cheek.
The last rose falls to the cold February ground.
The tall and proud trees, once calm, fiercely rustle with the cold autumn wind.
The sound of the leaves dancing on the cool air reminds me of the day we met.

How your voice so strong and triumphant defeated the breeze, which now resounds.
It's so faint, I can barely hear it now.
I close my eyes and grace my lips to remember
All those inconsistent memories form into an image of you.

The rain pours, erasing everything in sight.
These tears, my voice, all wiped clean.
Those words I wanted to say for you to hear
Linger on the tip of my tongue now unable to be heard.

I open my eyes, and all I see is the white sky and the tears it's shedding.
*"Ima mo aishiteiru,"** and I erase my sins in the continuing falling sadness.
I hide your memory in that narrow corridor between my eyelashes
In my most sincere attempt to protect you from your untimely death.

*Ima mo aishiteiru is Japanese for *Even now I love you.*

Mother Figure

(Dedicated to the late Minister Cheryl Maxine Herris)

Your hands were ones that were bathed in kindness and pain.
Although they were capable of giving out both, they administered love.
Love, which flowed over wrinkled black hands, hands that dried tears.

Love from which you let all walks of life drink from indiscriminately.
You bathed all of us in kindness at Showers of Blessing Ministries.

You did not judge others although they were ready to judge you,
Yet you saw past that and offered them the warmth of your Bible.
You perished while taking care of others; you are all of our mother.

*Sayonara** (No More Good-Byes)

Steps are not easily taken to overcome what we've gone through.
A distant star shined brilliantly on the path that leads me to you.
Your heart fell into my arms like snow; I tenderly grasp it with my hand
Only to watch it perish in these soiled hands, only leaning, no longer do I stand.

*Nieve*** was your nickname, and still I strongly desired to hold on to you.
Another moment passed, and you moved with it until I lost sight of you,
Remembering the fact that I was the footprint you left behind in the snow.
Another day in your absence, writing sayonara with kanji that spelled *woe*.

Sayonara is Japanese for *farewell*.
***Nieve* is Spanish for *snow*.

Ash

The ash pouring into the ashtray has a faint yet haunting glow.
As the candlelight fades and the sweet reminiscent smoke lingers,
We try to talk, to communicate, but all of our words are burned up.

The poison that clouds your lungs seems to taint your words.
Your tears you tried to cry are burned up like the ash.
The smoke that lingers suffocates us both.

I look out to you and ask why life can't be this simple,
And your image is engulfed in the smoke, this ash.
When we can't see eye to eye, we only scorn each other.

"Please don't light that cigarette; it's burning us both until there is nothing left."
The dull and tasteless bed we lay in is enveloped in ash.
The ash that falls like snow blankets the window sill.

I reach out to you, and my hands are singed.
I am the moth that gravitates to you, my flame.
I hold on to you until that familiar warmth incinerates me.

This fire, this warmth that was once so much you
Proceeds to rage wildly and encroach upon our past
Until there is nothing left of any one of us but ash.

When Tears Aren't Enough (Manuel Garza IV)

(In loving memory of the loveable Manual Garza IV.)

Your pink lips that were thick and stretched wide to reveal your smile
Have grown cold and dyed purple, signifying you lost your ability to smile.
When many of us were told you had died, we felt no pain but disbelief.
Your steps would not come again, and you lay falling earthbound like a leaf.

When tears aren't enough to bring the one we knew back,
And silence is filled with the sounds of hearts breaking; heart attack.

You see, I never saw you as dead because I can still remember the day that we met.
How I stumbled over you; I'd give up so much for those moments to be kept.
So many funny, anxious, and boring moments that we all let slip by
Over thoughts that we can't make new ones; we lay here still paralyzed.

When tears aren't enough to bring the one we loved back,
And we struggle to rebuild memories from the amount of time we lack.

You're dressed up, clean cut in a purple long-sleeve button-up dress shirt
But see that I remember your black shirt, blue jeans, and pretty girls whom you'd flirt.
I remember you being called Greed by Chris Porter, Jasmine, Jen, and Ralph Willis.
Now there is no more time for that, and on things like this we are forced to reminisce.

When tears aren't enough to bring the one who made us laugh back with a dare,
A dare to rise and shock us by telling us you wanted to prank all of us here.

You aren't dead to us, and none of us are in that state of disbelief or denial.
The actions, feelings, birthday surprises remind us of how you blessed us for a while.
When I know a thousand hugs won't make you come back or feel any better,
Know that it was your love and energy that now brings us together.
Know that you live tough in our skin like leather.

Foot Fetish

I am your feet; you walk both with me and on me.
Together we stroll through unpaved roads of uncertainty
As well as scurry across bustling cities of commercial monotony.

I am your feet, your reliable physical-support system.
I carry you forward without the need of your limbic system.
We dance complicated dances together, steps taken both inside and within.

I am your feet, forgotten on most days until I riddle you with pain.
Unaware of how I suffered under your weight and physical strain.
You walk on me not with me, unappreciated until I am gone.

No Hope for Phone Calls

Promising picture messages and tantalizing texts appear valuable in context,
But all these things lack the singular quality that could make you my next.
I greet you on mornings with sincere words and have developed a routine of it,
But it appears to me you seldom return answers or replies to most of it.

I let the dial tone I hear signify my attempt at creating something with you,
But you don't appreciate it because in hindsight there were things you never knew.
You weren't aware of the vast quantities of suitors seeking my phone number.
How they all had hoped that we could spend cold December nights together.

I would rather hear the differentiating tone and pitches in your voice
Instead of being falsely led to believe that I was your first choice.
You leave me no hope for phone calls, and in its place I find love withdrawals.
So please don't try and get in contact with me when you find out I ball.

Airplanes

Please don't trip off me; I am a passenger not a travel agency.
That baggage you wear is holding us back: travel-delay expectancy.
You were so fly before back when I had first known you,
But now you let your wings get clipped from cheap rendezvous.

You're stuck in an emotional snowstorm, grounded and unable to take passengers,
And I'm sorry to bring this news to you, but please don't shoot me, the messenger.
I came here to board you and protect you like an air marshall on flights,
But your baggage has you weighed down, pushing out others from fright.

Though I knew that waiting on you may lead to a long layover
And that I carried my own baggage, I just hoped my love letters you'd carry over.
You trip because you care and travel away from me for fear of falling
But know that I'll catch you, and your name I'll keep calling.

Punish justly those who have wronged you and up your airport security,
But fill yourself up with confidence and let love be your deputy.
You are so fly, so let go of your baggage and all that's hurting you.
Let those memories and people leave as though they were parachutes on board of you.

Typewriters

Ex-lovers' hands like typewriters imprint stories onto my skin,
Inscribing volumes in great depth, making them echo within.
My skin is dark parchment for them to leave their tales.
Both memories and experiences become tucked into this page like holding cells.

These people, like potential authors, seek publication of their manuscripts,
Claiming them to be groundbreaking yet plagiarizing from familiar hieroglyphs.

We self-publish these *novelas** unable to edit them,
Filling them with passion, love, dates, ticket stubs, and sin.

Their keys diligently press and continue to let their errors repeat,
Persisting proudly, expecting a standing ovation, refusing to take a seat.
When their stories are finished and the last sentence is complete and dotted,
I am abandoned and left with their finished work titled "Broken Hearted."

**Novelas* is Spanish for *novels* or *stories*.

Time Line

Angels could not give me the words to define
The beauty of this moment that we share in time.
It's amazing how memories and emotions can fill
Someone up with the urge to share a forbidden kiss.
To steal a moment in the past just to savor it in the present
Even in the face of knowing there will be no future.

In the brief and silent moments that are filled with quiet ticks,
I ask myself, "Is pain the only proof that we had once loved?"
And I let my eyes close, hiding the brilliance of this scene from them.
I must learn to accept that filling my hands with past bonds
Will leave me unable to grasp future possibilities.
Even if presently what I seek stands in front of me.

The strength it takes to resist touching, holding, and kissing you
When you pull me into the shadows of your sister's room for privacy.
The weakness it takes to let these moments of morality and indecisiveness
Cripple me, leaving me watching them as I construct a time line.
I lay still, quietly waiting and watching the sunrise as its light splashes over you
And sedate myself with writing as my body craves to be over you.

Time is not kind to me only, choosing to reveal its secrets only in hindsight.
I toil around in this ration of time afforded to me and surrender to its might.
I am an emotional tsunami wiping out those in passing bits of sorrow,
Seeking tranquility in you, my Poseidon, covered in the light of tomorrow.
Size-eighteen feet clumsily walk forward into a space that cannot be filled,
And I let my hesitation bind me, and my momentum is quieted and killed.

"We cannot last forever, but I would love to try to. As solitude disappears, and I spend
time with you."

Borracho

¡Toma todo, toma rápido, toma y olvida todo!
El olor de alcohol te adhieres a tu cuerpo flaco
En ese momento vive en un mundo ilustre
Aunque estuvo borracho la primera noche que nos encontramos, te pierdo…

¡Baila con la noche, baila con los otros negros, baila y olvida me!
El sonido de botellas rompiendo mientras sus labios besan les.
En ese momento vive en un mundo sin luz, adonde la noche nunca parar,
Aunque mi corazón esta borracho mi cerebro esta sobrio, y me pierdes

¡Llora por ellos, llora por amor, llora y olvida todo que te duelen!
El sentimiento de miedo y tristeza que toman y bailan contigo,
En ese momento vive en el mundo que quieres, sin realidad.
Aunque me conoces, nunca te conozco sin el sabor de alcohol atrás de tus labios.

¡Olvida la manera que te aman, olvida mis besitos, olvida mis brazos!
El presión de pasando tiempo contigo es que me mataste,
En ese momento vive en el mundo separado de me.
Aunque te recuerdo, no nadie puede cambiar el pasado que nos compartimos.

Breathe

People are like breaths of air.
They can fill you with love or despair.
They come and go with each push
Not leaving much to cherish,
Yet without them we'd perish.

We may find ourselves racing,
Rushing through life not pacing.
Trying too hard to grab onto something,
To find our chest left filled with nothing.

There is but one simple and enduring remedy
For this most venomous toxicity
And that is to accept that the next breath is not guaranteed.
To find beauty, hope, hate, and love in the creation of the deed
And that sometimes we just have to remember to breathe is all we need.

Glimmer (Luera)

My cell phone's light lit up this dark room,
And for a while, I stared at the images of you.
I used to ask, "Is pain the only proof that we have loved?"
As the light on my phone slowly fades to black.

The more I try to love you, the more masochistic I become.
You never led me on, especially when I was by your side.

There is little warmth in holding on to this,
Yet there is more than there was before.
My eyelids grow heavy with doubt and shut themselves.
That way, the lack of light in the room will go unnoticed.

The more I try to love you, the more masochistic I become.
But still, you never hurt me intentionally; no you never did.

I wanted to be the one that you would cry to, who could heal you.
I can admit that it was selfish of me when so many needed you.
I know not how long I can endure this on my own.
When the only time I hear you is by listening to your voice mail.

The more I love you, the more masochistic I become.
But still, I loved everything you gave me, no matter how small.

My ear is a cave that is waiting idle for the familiarity of your voice,
But all it hears is the ring, ring, ringing of an unanswered phone.
My phone vibrates, and light begins to fill the room
Only to reveal the condensation of emotions I have.

Rain

Droplets of condensed emotion blanket the city.
Cold harmonies both spill and sing over the valley.
Nourishment is conjured in the hands of strangers and familiars.
The tea kettle's steam softens the seal on an unmarked envelope.

The clouds come together though waiting to kiss;
Our fingers locked together like mixed-colored shoelaces.
Rainfall pitter-patters on our umbrella as we walk together
With both uneven yet in-sync footsteps down a new path.

We were soaked in each other's sweat
As we laid down and mimicked the rain as it crept.
You let me pour myself over you, and our limbs interlock
As we touch each other, and you search for something hard, rock.

We were soaked in each other's tears when the rain stopped.
We let go of like and love as well as us as we separated.
I was left confined to my home, praying for thunderstorms to come.
The clouds have poured everything they had out and dispersed quietly.

Memories of these moments in the rain become lost;
Old feelings begin to heat up with anger and evaporate.
The space you created when I accepted your good-bye
Has collapsed upon itself, and the letter dissolves.

I Hate You

I hate how my shower is never hot enough in your absence.
I can't help but miss how your kisses lingered on me like fingerprints.
It was so much like a crime, and we both saw your residue.

I hate how you had a way to make time stand absolutely still,
The way you kept me up and focused like a Viagra pill.

I hate how *I love you* doesn't feel the same when it's not off your lips.
Your love was real deep, nine inches deep.
Something hard to handle that would awaken me from sleep.

I hate how your *I love you* always sounded like *good-bye*,
Yet in the morning you would lay kisses on me as we lie.

I hate how I still hear your soft whispers over the wind,
How the neighbors still ask about you, over all the time we spent.
I hate how you let me put it down but still lifted me up.

I hate you for making me forget who I was and what it meant to *Do me*.
It's easy to understand why, though, when I was so busy doing you.

I hate you for giving me something to hold on to but not to own.
I hate you for late-night and early morning alarms, a sex-found moan.
I was your favorite slow jam you played on Repeat, yet you did cheat.

Angels (Without Wings)

You who foolishly tried to flatter angels
Now unashamedly demonize me.
You fluttered your eyes as though mimicking butterflies,
And I felt those tempestuous feelings, butterfly effect.

I waited for time to collapse upon itself
And let everything that these human hands constructed
Become ruined, turned to nothing more than particles of dust.

I who could not tell the difference between
I love you and your *Good-bye*
As demons carve at my heart, creating an urn.

I craved a place without ceilings or skies and remembered
Emily Dickson once said, "Hope is a thing with wings,"
Yet mine were prematurely clipped by your hands.
These are the words of an angel without wings.

Those tempestuous emotions uplift me, and I experience transcendence.
Without wings I fly to that place that offered a glimmer of you.
Within this continuously falling rain, I whispered, "I hate you."

My tongue played with words to tell you
Only to choke on them as you had my other gifts.
I wanted to uplift you even without wings.

I hear the sound of wing beats as I try to gather myself,
Carefully reconstructing all that you had left of me.
Though I am unable to lift you who I cherished up,
I can do myself a favor and push you away from me.

Fuck Love

I wanted to be your pillow and give you a warm place for you to rest,
But your actions and lack of words got me sicker than a positive blood test.
I put good faith in you and made you a priority for my loving actions,
But you left me on the back burner and considered me a distraction.

You're the reason why people "smash or pass" over "love and cherish"
Because shallow interactions leave you thirsty, and love soon begins to perish.
I started to write a few lines of love poetry for you that are left unfinished.
You were meant to be an inspiration for me, yet you gave me nothing to replenish.

So I will spit this lyrically for a moment, and forgive me for this, Father.
For my anger over being deprived of infatuation, of being called Pa like his father.
I'm saying fuck love with emphasis on the exclamation mark
Because you got me paranoid and uncertain; question mark!

I'm going to spend time and money on myself lavishly
And protect myself from all of those like you with psychology.
It's a little bit whatever though maybe one day we can be acquaintances,
So next time I won't paint your walls white like billboard canvasses.

Let me calm down a moment and say I wish you happiness
But do in time realize that it is not on the tip of different penises.
You will love and be given love from a variety of men;
Just keep it friendly until you can allocate time to spend.

You can decide how you present yourself to others, my friend.
I just hope that all of this good love you gave was not pretend.
I'm just going to say fuck love and shorten its life expectancy
By tattooing on my heart the words *self-love* and *celibacy*.

Thank You; I'm Sorry; I Love You; Good-bye

I am left with few words to say to you,
So it is best to say them now before they lose their power.

Thank you for the reply text and the mix tape,
All the little things we did leading up to our last date.
You offered words of warmth and concern for my health
And invested something precious in value to us: wealth.

Thank you for trying even when you were too tired,
For taking my breath away and leaving me inspired.

I'm sorry for crude jokes and emotional bouts,
Traumatic experiences that filled you with doubts.
I'll never fully grasp the damage I dealt
Nor will you of all the neglect I felt.

I'm sorry for being a bit much at times yet never really enough;
How I endured to find value in your eyes like a diamond in the rough.

I love you with every inch and every part of my heart that I gave.
I both foolishly and selfishly tried to be so much to you: support enclave.
I realized I admired both your fleeting warmth and constant coldness;
I loved how we could briefly encompass both of these with fondness.

I loved you romantically for being all that you were, your true self.
So I shall place this lost love for you next to the pages about you on my bookshelf.

Good-bye to you my Rio, my Ai, my glimmer of light.
For the one I was falling for but who could not hold me at night.
I accept your farewell that you nicknamed Friendship.
As I close my eyes and sink, "You sunk my battleship!"

Good-bye "Good morning" text, lukewarm afternoons, and cold lonely nights
As all remain unfinished in this new time called twilight.

I am left with few words for you, so it's best to say them now,
"Thank you; I'm sorry; I love you; Good-bye."

You Promised

I sift through memories like grains of sand that keep slipping.
You were the type to never leave anything behind, yet I kept tripping.

When love exists only in dreams, so I rush quickly to sleep,
Spending limited time together only to wake up and weep.
It's hard knowing I can rest eternally with you with a sleeping pill,
One that promises to keep me asleep until dreams are all that is real.

You promised that when a thousand could not make my pain vanish
That you would be the one thousand and one for me to cherish.

As I wear my glasses, it is your promise that I keep in mind:
That whenever I wear them to think of you and, "To be more kind."
Yet even as I wear them, it is your face that I can't seem to find.

You promised to use the strength in your arms to protect,
But now you and your arms are six feet under, and there is no strength left.

If my most genuine wish comes true, it would be to stop your death.
The coldness felt by your absence is all that is left.
*"Yo siento depresivo y no te veo,"** yet I look for you.
Now all I can say is, *"Ima mo obetieru."*****

*Yo siento depresivo y no te veo is Spanish for *I feel depressed, and I can't see you.*
**Ima mo obetieru is Japanese for *Even now I remember you.*

Chapter III: Identity in Love

Congratulations are in order as you have been able to read this far into this book. This section focuses on the complications of love and those feelings of infatuation that we have all been exposed to. If you have yet to feel the warmth of love's embrace or a lack of it, I promise that you will find warmth in these words that follow this brief introduction.

I ask that you remember that *love* is defined by the people who create it—not by others. With this in mind, please find your own definition of *love*. Also remember that

"You are someone's definition of *love*."

The color of this chapter is that of orange. Orange can represent enthusiasm and creativity whenever it is present. In this same sense, we typically become enthusiastic about future prospects of love and of those who may love us. We must also remain creative in our endeavor and steadfast to maintain and create something better than what was there before.

Love

Love is not toiling in between bed sheets.
Love makes hearts create rhythm: hip-hop beats.
Now as it falls in my eyes, love is a myth.
Perhaps love is an ancient folktale from a hieroglyph.

I have heard that love has the power to make hearts sing,
To push together two separate individuals to a vow; wedding ring.
What I know is that love has left me with many sad songs to sing,
With no returned phone calls, and unanswered dial tones left to ring.

I am no scholar of this interdisciplinary love issue,
But I have felt its grace and felt need for a tissue.
I am not one who sports their love of being single
But behind closed doors searches for others with whom to mingle.

If love is anything that I can be aware of or know,
Then love is parents and friends watching us grow.
Love is a whirlwind, which sweeps us swiftly off our feet,
Then leaves our heart pounding again: hip-hop beats.

Estoy Enamorado*

I sit in the hospital room listening to the sound of life-support beeps and nurse's heels
And feel the cold breeze from opening sliding doors tickle me, a feeling surreal.
A slight glance into the past reveals to me memories of various important lovers,
So many who could see past what I was and did not have fear that I'm a brother.

Is it weird or rather beautiful to remember those simple things of the past
Like the way he held my hand or how deeply I wanted our evening kiss to last?
I don't know if it's good or not to have this complex and lovely feeling,
But simply put, I rest assured in this act as a sign I am healing.

Plainly put, I am in love with the past for the tragedy that it could not last.
The beauty, grace, and tranquility of something that is not eternal
Allows for me to invest in sweet dreams, not those sad and ephemeral.
The secret kisses, the good-morning messages, and the multitude of phone calls.

I don't know if it's okay to have this feeling, but I'm happy to have it
Even if I am filled with this feeling while they are absent.
Plain and simply, I am in love with the past, for the possibility it could last.
I am looking forward to cheating on it, regardless of past features, with my future.

Estoy enamorado is Spanish for *I'm in love.*

This Will Be (Our Last Night Together)

The candle fire burns and fades in a dark room with its light.
Although I am anxious and shivering at my decision, this isn't fright.
The thought of us meeting together like this simply disgusts me.
So though your lips look inviting, I wish for them to be free.

I want to make poetry with you not for you.
I'd rather demonstrate than tell you I adore you.
Don't trip off me unless you have your luggage packed
Because, baby, you're fly; no need for a jet pack.

You got me pushing bike pedals just to ride out and see you,
Finding clever ways of expressing myself for you to see through.
I'm confused and lost over the many promises you never made or spoke,
But you put thoughts to action as we laid and never left me hanging: rope.

The candlelight burns out, and this will be our last night together
Because we stand here as individuals, sharing both moments and weather;
And in this thought it sickens me, for you not once resorted to promiscuity.
So I want to end this feeling of individuality and meld us together; you feel me?

This will be our last night together as two separate individuals
Because in these following moments we will be made whole.
I want to be a new part of your world in which for you to discover;
I want to be the one who nestles with you underneath the cover.

I Miss You

I am lost in thoughts of sounds and voices alike,
And at new and approaching emotions, I develop fright.
Yes fear and excitement are two sides of the same coin,
And yes it took courage to flip it, but for you, I decided to risk it.

I don't like this feeling of unshakeable uncertainty,
Yet I find comfort refreshing my memory of him and me.
I find myself filling free time with words to dedicate to you; end rhyme.

I dislike this feeling of craving your presence;
I like being surrounded by you covered in your essence.
On our first date, you picked me up, and we cooked for each other,
And within a few hours of talking, I wouldn't seek another.

I don't like admitting that I like the thought of spending time together.
I like the concept of viewing your smile under any varying weather.
I find myself with moments to contemplate what we will do on our next date.

I am lost in thought of scents, movies, and *Family Guy*.
Of watching it together while on my stomach you would lie.
I dislike the fact that I miss you but love that I do,
So keep in touch with me; help connect me to you.

December

I was a child born in winter
Whose eyes caught glimpse of a pure-white sky.
The snowflakes elegantly falling
Resembled the flowers of spring
Dancing timelessly on a morning breeze.

I grasp the distant flake as it lies upon my hand.
So beautiful, so fragile, it quickly fades away.

I don't mourn over its departure as I take my journey home.
The cold, harsh winds are comforting.
As I open the door, the warm, radiant light greets me,
Reminding me I'm home in your arms.
My fingertips once frigid held tightly in your hands
So soft, so tender; I slip away into your arms.

There is no reason to go outside to make snow angels
When there's one holding my hand right now.

With your fingers, you touched the frosted window.
You wrote out so many things.
As a child born in winter, all I would see was snow,
But right now you're my spring, the warmth that clings to me.
You lie in my arms drifting to sleep,
Gazing at these happy tears I weep.

Chi Hullo Li

Chi hullo li means *I love you.*
It is the beauty of this word I give you.
The vocal chords come from the Choctaw language.
They are flavored, sweetened, and tempered with age.

Yes these soft lips spoke *I love you* in Chatah Anumpa.
They promise you rich nourishment; no need to call Ma or Pa.
These are words of comfort and sustenance.
They are injected and overlaced in that love substance.

Chi hullo li means *I love you.*
It means no one else stands before you here or above you.
No one else has traversed the two-year path you have taken,
So prepare to hear them on every morning that next to me you awaken.

Amor

Los rayos del sol pintan el cielo azul con sus dedos vivios,
En uno respiro te digo "Te amo para siempre."
Haciendo amor contigo es poesía,
Y es porque eres mis lagrimas, y mi sonrisa.

Los dolores que tienes son difíciles para eliminar solo,
Así compartir los conmigo no tengo miedo, y vaya dejar te solo.
No te pregunto para olvidar las cosas importantes a ti en el pasado,
Mi único deseo es para cambiar la clase de lágrimas que lloras.

Kimi Dake Wo*

Within these fragile, shifting moments that fall through our hands,
We let go of time in each other's presence, pouring out like hourglass sands.
Eyes flutter on the edge of space, exchanging mixed messages of desires to procure,
Investing in the exchange of a kiss that carries more than simple moisture.

Sheets of ice cover the car window that lay decorated with our handprints.
As you close your eyes, I whisper, "*Watashi koto dake wo*"** in moments.
The world captured in the lens of your eye is uniquely yours;
It is the soft, gentle, creeping silence found after intercourse.

Within that space known as the edge of time,
In which you lay your head next to mine,
Stumbled out the words "*Kimi Dake Wo*,"
Ignoring both our fears that this moment would go.

Kimi Dake Wo is Japanese for *Only you.*
**Watashi koto dake wo* means *Look only at me.*

Rebirth

As I clumsily step out the shower to open the door,
In this moment soaked in readiness, I saw you, whom I adore.
The first breath I take in your presence is one of new life.
You heal wounds that others left in my back with a knife.

In the time it took to meet you, I discarded who I was,
Becoming hollow and refilling myself with your love.

It was not that I was dead before we met or before you came.
I was simply another stranger's plaything with a cute face and forgettable name.
You are the first face that I see, the first thing that appears dear to me.
This is my rebirth, a discovery made in your eyes called worth.

In the distance it took to cross and stand right in front of you,
I learned to say to my good friend Loneliness, "Adieu."

You are the first lips I kiss and do cherish.
The first to comfort me when I am embarrassed.
As you step forward just a few more feet from the miles you cross,
We embrace the tenderness, and my pain, sorrow, and heartache are lost.

Early Morning Prayer

I wake up just five minutes before you do
And watch as the sunrise greets the morning dew.
I get on my knees and pray to prepare myself for you.
My words first travel from my heart to my mind, not impromptu.

I thank God for putting me through all this to enjoy this morning view.
I wait for that simple shrug of your shoulder telling me you're awake.
I sit on my knees not wanting to please but confide in it and find peace.

Words flow like song lyrics off my tongue to increase potency.
Songs become wordless, and I praise him in evocable language in which I lack fluency.
To give thanks to those family members and loved ones who walked before me
Through miraculous event and much adversity, gave me life, and this morning glory.

My heart is a monument to my creators and forbearers.
Through my morning prayer, I learn how to lie next to you, my comfort layer.
My arms lay on top of you, cradling you just before you wake.
I close my eyes and hold you, my prayer, giving you my breath to take.

Sueño*

The quiet dream that crept slowly into my bed
Has unveiled a picture I had once forgotten on these summer days.
The cold breeze that sweeps through this house chills us both,
Making me draw you near, where my heartbeats you can hear.
You are like *un sueño*; you are beautiful and solely mine.

If only for one night…
As I awaken among a field of soiled bedsheets alone,
I grasp sincerely on to that last memory left in this room.
That lone shard, which was held tightly in these hands.
Now a river of blood pours slowly over these dry hands,
And it erases yesterday's deeds and that last dream.

If only for one night…
Wounds that heal quickly leave lessons unlearned.
As I close my eyes on another cold night and let go,
Your soft breath begins to tickle my neck as you enter.
So calm and steady your heart beats as my heart races,
Races until it collapses from fatigue, and I fall again into your arms.

If only for one night…
*Los sueños que nos compartimos ahorita nos dejan,***
And even in my waking breath I know that it escapes me.
I still cling to that hope that the next morning we shall share.
Even without my *Respiro*** and without my *Estrella*,****
My eyes close slowly, waiting for another passerby.

If only for one night…
Before that last conscious breath escapes me,
Before my eyes lose their will to open themselves,
My lips press against your head as I hold you tightly.
I sing a familiar melody, humming for both of us delightfully,
"Mr. Sandman bring me a dream; make her the cutest that I've ever seen."

Sueño is Spanish for *Dream*.
**Los sueños que nos compartimos ahorita nos dejan* is Spanish for *The dreams we shared had left us*. ****Estrella* is Spanish for *Star*
****Respiro* is Spanish for *Breath*.

Respiro*

Lying in bed with thoughts of you floating around my head,
The smell of you lays heavy with me as you once did.
That first breath I take that wakes me is you, my *respiro*.
The laziness that fills this quiet afternoon brings me nostalgia.

Sleeping on top of my roof on a somber spring day,
My *respiro* warms me as gloomy rain clouds drift away.
Reaching out for the next breath, hand held tightly to my chest,
And letting go of the last; with you in my arms, my heart's at rest.

Getting up today, washing your laziness away, I embrace the sun
For giving me another day with you for which I have won.
You are my first and last *respiro* that I chose to take,
Falling asleep in your arms, I pray to never wake.

For if I should slumber among *tus brazos fuertes*** and forget who I am,
Then in your eyes, my identity shall forever stand.
If I should fall into a coma with your kisses just like soma,
Then sweet dreams shall ravish me of you, and I shall forever be.

Respiro is Spanish for *breath*.
***Tus brazos fuertes* is Spanish for *your strong arms*.

Aura

Sitting with friends on a fresh summer night,
Watching the moon hang over the water.
The ripples in the river reflecting the moonlight
Look like shining stars shimmering in the night sky.

If your presence is the moon, then my heart is the tide,
Drawing me in and letting me go like ebb and flow.

Ever reflecting your face in my shallow waters,
A tear rolls down my cheek, and in a soft sigh
Those words came stumbling out,
I love you.

One Thousand Nights

Over a thousand nights and words I've written to you.
I don't want to give up hope for tomorrow,
So I look into your eyes today, hoping the radio will play
That song that gives this feeling meaning.

Over a thousand nights and words I've wandered.
When did simple moments that started with,
"I love you" and ended with your smile
Fade into times when I needed to ask you,
"Do you even care?" and you reply with a sigh.

Over a thousand nights and words I've used to say, "I love you."
I honestly believe that I'm sincere.

Over a thousand nights and words I've heard.
The sound of the radio as you touch the dial,
Searching for that song that won't play.
The song that gave this feeling meaning,
The song that contained the words *I love you*.

Umbrella (Part 2)

Umbrellas pop up like flowers in spring,
Showered with love from the rain above.
Below lovers huddle close.
Cold breath and warm kisses infatuate the soul.

The sound of the windchimes so elegant;
That song is still being played in the rain.

After the rain, the light appears, and in the evening sky the moon shines pure.
Being captured by love's embrace is a new and awkward feeling.
The umbrellas that bloom like flowers offer protection from rain showers.
Guard the little tenderness that is kept in between the heat of two people.

Maichiru*

Cherry blossoms blanket the ground like snow.
The spring winds tickle your neck.
Your eyes, which seemed to look out to the world's brilliant color,
Seem to have become much colder from sitting in the dark.

The flowers' colors are still there even if you can't see them now.
Your delicate fingers, which tried so hard to sow these flowers that bloom around us,
Can they still remember the touch of the softest petals?
You used to say, "Spring is such a short time," but winter's far off.

Remember the way the first day of school was
When you walked through the crowd to see your precious flowers bloom?
Don't let go of that moment no matter what happens.
"In the dark there is a little light; just look for it,
And when you find it, you'll find me."

"I'll still be there under the willow tree."

*Maichiru is Japanese for *Dance Step* or *Fluttering Step*.

Toki (Time)

I cannot repair a broken promise,
But if I could reach across time,
I would connect your heart to mine.

Not by a single ribbon or a thread
But by the vows we speak
On our way to our wedding bed.

I can't ask for time as we swim through it.
All I can do is piece together the promise bit by bit.
I'll find the last piece and make it fit.
Even if we don't have forever, we still have time.

A Song for Kimmi and Chu

As old love fades away with yesterday's distant memories,
In the distance I saw you for the first time.
The sun's brilliant light glowed off of your resilient body.
Those first words you spoke brought spring to me.

Winter's cold hands could no longer reach me, as you drew me close for the first time.
The moments felt right as they passed by.
Time in your arms seemed to stand still.
You didn't need to say too much of anything to express your love.

Your tender love, your enduring love, this love that I can't shake away.
How it feels so familiar, like a mother's warm apple pies sitting on the kitchen table.
I know you'll be there as the seasons change.
When winter comes again, you'll be my warmth.

Sheltering me from the storm that is life
As you hold me close and our lips press for the first time.
Everything I've known and loved seems to go into that moment
Where the scent of the spring flowers lingered on your jacket.
The warmth of the sun and the cool-blue summer sky are mine.

Love Letters

Your hands they shake as they tear the sealed paper.
The words inscribed cause your body to tremble.
Your lips and fingertips grow excited as you read each line.
This is a feeling only in love letters you can find.
These words that carry meaning dig deeper than any other
To a place that had not been previously discovered.

Love letter, love letter
What are you telling me tonight?
Love letter, the scent of the person who last wrote lingers,
Bringing you closer to them.
So much closer until your lips press,
And now you're speechless.

Love letter, so beautiful inside where your words and feelings can hide.
The arms of the writer reach out to you from a distant land and
Are just holding on, yes holding on to you tenderly tonight.
This is my love letter, reaching out to you, so don't cry!
As the words begin to leave the pages in which they were held,
I embrace you with the hands that crafted this love for you.

Tennis Courts

A typical August afternoon, and we're lying in the wet grass by the courts.
The sound of rackets smashing, of players panting have all but vanished.

The slightest breeze offers relief, and the trees protect us from the sun.
The shadows of the trees gather around us and watch as we lie in peace.

The quiet moment ends as sound returns from ringing school bells.
Summer is at its end, and we are both full of summer tales.

I see you the next morning by the tennis courts; your racket rises with the sun,
And I lean against the rusty gate as time pauses and you're about to serve.

The person I admire being trapped in the first words that I write,
That moment that you're about to take, and I witness is my delight.

Promise

The winter's raindrops roll off the leaves of withered flowers.
A breath of cool air brings me down to a world where I'm welcome.
I can't escape your memory even in this world I built in solitude.

My gentle words are still ringing in your head as we hold on to this moment.
Maybe you didn't understand it then; you always wondered what I meant.
But now more than then, it's truer now than it ever had been.

The light from the sun seems to dance upon the descending leaves.
Every moment seemingly dies and is reborn into the next,
Each moment more unique and more beautiful, as you were.

So I'm telling you now as you lay with me confused as it had seemed,
Let your wings unfold and fly out to the things we have dreamed.
I'll keep my end of that promise we made, as I am determined.

Whispers of the Moon

I sit on a stranger's porch on an arid summer night.
Tears fill my eyes, clinging to them like dew to roses.
My broken finger traces the outline of my heart,
And the moon begins to sing me a lullaby.
The first lyric was your name.

The wind rustles the leaves of the canopy, and harmony is made.
The seas of sorrow and sadness made tranquil.
My heart's beat is the instrument that first cord was strung on.
Your words and the image behind them is what I hung on.

While leaning against the windowsill, the fall winds embrace me.
I heard the moon sing a single word that captivated me.
A lyric of the lullaby it sang was your name.
As I sit underneath that silver shifting ring of light,
I let my soul embrace you, my musical delight.

Migration of Butterflies (Ode to James)

I heard a butterfly's wing beat.
It was quiet at first and in moments of silence did retreat.
The sole spark, which gave birth to such a creature,
Was no striking or prominent, attractive feature.

It was birthed from the warmth of your hand.
A simple bond welded romantically like a ceremonial band.

I felt the pressure of a solitary pair of wings flap
As the rhythm to Beyoncé's "Halo" on my arm you did tap.
You would not let me hasten our first kiss,
And I know when it comes, it's guaranteed bliss.

Sanchito

Two years we have filled with words of comfort when needed.
Words of love that others could not decode; deep seated.
Your heart was fertile ground for me to plant a lone seed
That would blossom into a fruit called love to feed your need.

You live in a place so very far away, and it is there I hide you, my heart, away.
Within the comfort of your eyes, I lose care for labels like *straight* or *gay*.
You helped rebuild me in times where I felt isolated,
Kept me from focusing too much on green when I could have become jaded.

We met on Thanksgiving, and it was this meeting that I was thankful for.
We spent a whole day together, and you kept craving me, more and more.
So we nestled together on a playground swing, strangers becoming intimate.
No longer so distant, I held you tightly in my arms, making a new covenant.

You cried in my arms while I sang to you, my voice accompanied by the steady
And excited beat of my heart as I held you in my arms tight like a teddy.
If I had known from Adam for Adam we would start.
I'd know that you would never leave me with a broken heart.

Golden arches of the Bay Area have invited and are waiting for us
Even if we have to try different ways to get there and reach each other, maybe bus?
You're my Paulywhirl, and I think you will evolve into a Paultytoad,
Betraying your dedication is something my heart has forebode.

First Love

I kept a story tucked intimately within the corridors of my heart.
In moments of pain and happiness, I did turn to it to draw light.
Through the distance and unfamiliarity, of which this story was written,
I wished to send you the comfort of the thousands of fleeting words.

Time has aged this silly piece of parchment and dyed it yellow.
Both fragile to touch and weak, it holds strength in its crevasses.

I first began to write what I had lost long before I could understand
What I had gained and to what extent I was both teacher and student.
I had begun to tuck away the things I wished to say to you tightly onto a lost page.
Things that your wisdom and my heart had both forbade.

Time has given me both worlds and words to toil and struggle with,
And in your absence, I have found many different endings.

I let words creep out of my mouth and onto these pages.
Like secrets, they were both enticing and private but still yours.
Things hidden from the public eye like five individual fingers
Dancing a waltz together as they make a held hand of both grace and charm.

Time has taken both tears of joy and love indiscriminately at its leisure.
Making the spine of this book stand tall and firm in your remembrance.
I am this book that I write, which has hidden many things from you.
My pages wish for you to read them and know my resounding voice.
Through both distance and time your hand has influenced mine.
A few blank pages left, and I wonder who will be the next verse.

Dilemma

Today a cold breeze swept across the cherry trees,
And I shuddered at the smell of your scent, taking a moment to think.
Do I dedicate words to you in rhyme such as those of poetry?
Perhaps in time will flow like song verses from groups like Floetry.

Is it better to ignore precious attempts at mad and lyrical flows
In favor of something less rhythmic than song, maybe prose?
Thoughts gradually subside into another like tides.
Fond memories of future and past joyrides.

I can't set in stone such dire and beautiful emotions,
But I can still say, "I love you" in a sincere tone and motions.
I find moments woven carefully into that epoch of time
And find grace in this well-aged gift like those from the grapevine.

I am thoughts trapped in a shell as eyes grow tear filled.
The waves turn violently in this hell, and love lies bleeding; killed.
It is to you this dearest and most fond memory,
I dedicate to you this afternoon's sweet reverie.

Midnight Shower

Awkward feet walk, stumble, and trip over each other into the shower,
As loving hands turn the knob in search of warmth and comfort.
Beads of hot liquid both bombard and soak me, relieving an emotional ride.
This liquid warmth gives my tears a place to dwell and hide.

Eyelids heavy with a day's exhaustion close themselves,
As water carves ledges on soft, unused lips.
Heavy-weighted doubt and uncertainty evaporate;
I look to my life and begin to rerate.

At this present moment, I am crushing on you, and therein lies the problem.
I've let that idea sneak inside of a crack not so easily repaired and now look solemn.
I am happy on more days than not and have grown so much in a small amount of time
But still selfishly turn over at the thought you possibly maybe could be mine.

I'm uncertain of today or tomorrow's unweighed action,
But for now I will smile and let your face be a distraction.
I am arms to love and hands to hold and cherish.
I am blessed from above, stand both tall and bold, and from this I shall not perish.

Yes I am crushing on you; it's both sad and funny but mainly true.
But as I step out the shower to these feelings I bid, "Adieu."
Awkward feet walk, stumble, and trip over each other out of the shower,
As loving hands caress one another, offering warmth and comfort.

Whirlwind

Whirlwind love sweeps me off my feet,
Carrying me away and leaving me stranded in strange places,
Often among a dozen or so hungry and unfamiliar faces.

Love was what I had chased after yet never had, no matter how fast I was.
However, love was like a fair-weather friend, vanishing as the winds pick up.
Love never had my back, but its sister lust did, offering me a quick pick-me-up.

Lust pretended to be my friend and hopped into my bed,
Painted falsehoods with words and homes made of empty promises in my head.
So I walk along an empty road with no one for my heart to abode.

Wild, tempestuous winds settle, and the steam from my heart blows off, tea kettle.
I stand amid the edge of a mountain with the wind blowing at my back.
I move forward as it dances at my heel, still searching for something real.

Worth the Wait

The value of something cannot be determined solely on the first date,
And although true love may be at first sight, for this we should wait.
Over heavy thoughts and past experience we must both contemplate.
If not knowing how the other feels as the moments pass, and we frustrate.

Something so easily obtained is easily devalued and unappreciated,
Painting optimistic lovers with shades of jealousy and loss; jaded.
Feelings of possible love lost over infatuation make us feel hated,
Perhaps used and confused over unfulfilled promises we debated.

As we lie in each other's arms and comforts while we can,
I refuse to knowingly walk in blind without the title of *your man*.
For I hold you to higher level than most, a set platform;
Although bodies both young and willing can perform.

Show me that betwixt your thighs lies heaven's gate
And that you haven't let anyone enter after a first date.
I want to know what your value is postsale by fate.
Let's prove to each other it's worth the wait.

Crown Royal

Hot August nights deprive me of moisture, and my lips remain dry.
As I experience exodus from my car, I catch a stranger's eye.
He wore caramel skin with eyelashes that mimicked the wings of butterflies.
He was not a tall glass of water but definitely a shot of something dark and wise.

His smooth words poured like Crown Royal into a shot glass and I over the edge.
I find warmth in this inebriation that sweeps me off my feet as he bites my cartilage.
He is the promise of fulfillment and I the desire he wishes to conquer.
He shoots down into your stomach quickly as though he intends for it to rupture.

His lips are my intoxication, something I considered myself immune to, vaccination.
I clumsily let a stranger in too close but do not slow down from hesitation.
I am stumbling, dizzy, falling and, like Elle Varner, I need a "Refill."
I push both myself and my virtue into bed solo to give myself time to heal.

I wake up hung over from the evening's deeds but still sharp to my wits.
I toss pillows and sheets over, looking for my ringing phone as if throwing hissy fits.
I find it and listen to the uneven beat of his unheard vocal chords;
Finding happiness and silliness in this, my first taste of dark liquor.

Moonlight

The radiance of the moon spilled out its luster and reflected itself in your eyes.
You were beckoning me closer until we both lay entrapped in each other's arms.
I promised that tomorrow would be yours; under the circumstances, today was ours.
These words I happily gave to you seem to find home within that crevice called your heart.

It is a calling that guides us both toward each other until both of our hearts connect,
And I can feel your uneven heartbeats as my lips begin to grace your neck.
As I give thanks to the moon for giving you to me tonight and grow lost in its light,
I close my eyes, and in the last moments before sunrise, I feel you pressed against me.

Chemistry

We are molecules of carbon and oxygen waiting to combust,
Hoping to give off water and erode our London-dispersion forces.
For the longest time we have been bonded similar to ionic compounds.
I freely gave away my electron to you, and this lead to redox reaction.

When I first met you, you were no noble gas stable and whole on your own.
You were so electronegative that I felt your pull, so attractive you took a part of me.
Still I struggled and stood by you, waiting patiently for that to change.
We are not covalently bonded, but I wouldn't mind sharing an electron with you.

Although there is pressure to stay together, the distance between us is too great.
With limited resources to draw from, the warmth we had is now absolute zero.
We meet one last time as your electronegativity draws me in for this precious moment.
Warmth builds up, volume decreases, and pressure increases until we explode: fireworks!

Love in Stages (For the Ages)

Puppy love is that tender and uninhibited love that is found in childhood,
Painted by awkward first kisses and the joy of youthful promises all made good.
It is in that early, elementary love that elderly in hindsight make fun of.
It is playground swings and trivial things; yes, this is pure puppy love.

First love is that intense hormonal rage that puts the world onto a newfound stage.
It's like teenage movies that draw two lovebirds together and entrap them; cage.
When the nice guy fails and the bad boy prevails, a contradiction to story tales.
Every song of heartbreak on the radio is about us, so we sing like nightingales.

Adult love found in between that time of renting apartments to owning a house.
Love found in conquering our past fears as a lion, no longer a timid mouse.
Suitors becomes aware of the baggage she has with her and pursue her.
Eyes settle, understand, and accept as they see beauty in how they perceive her.

Eternal love is found within that elder age with a lifetime of memories to keep,
And loyalty is held even at the fear it will all end with that last life-support beep.
It is the beauty that feet have traveled long distances over road-map skin in sync.
That we are mortal and that this last form of love is not something that leaves us in a
blink.

Transcendence

I am pins and needles on how to carefully define this.
At the moment, I am left incapable of this and left speechless.
There is wonder in not having the words and just having the expression.
To be caught in the moment by Father Time and being taught a lesson.

I want to make something more beautiful than love
With someone that I love more than my own life.

I don't know how it got this way, but I don't care.
How I could be kneeling with my eyes heavy, then become suspended in the air.
What is this serene grace that will not flee when I see your face?
My shoes were so worn down from pursuit, yet it was for me you gave chase.

I want to make something more physical than love
With someone that knows my spirit and heart like God.

I can't comprehend the childish excitement that is found in this joy
That has my eyes and intentions hidden from you as I smile and play coy.
What is this warmth that adheres to me like a hug that just won't go away?
My heart hadn't fallen in love yet, but it was submerged in it today.

I want to make something more poetic than love
With someone whose scent clings to me more than my own.

I am an amateur writer using words to capture something I can't name.
It grows and spreads within me, both heating and lifting me up like propane.
What is this softness that's gentler than a kiss from mother onto my cheek?
My heart, body, soul, mind, shoes, and feet are all begging that this stays on Repeat.

You Being You

Can we pretend that I'm your knight in shining armor, and you're my Prince Charming
So that when either one of us falls in love it will be without warning?
Can I be the one who comforts you late night on the end of the telephone receiver,
So when your mom says, "I think you love this boy," you undoubtedly believe her?

Can I hear you whisper my name softly into my ear
As I make a commitment to you, my career?
Is it odd or beautiful that "You being you" inspires me
Even when I have yet to traverse the world that is you entirely?

Can I get a kiss from you and maybe steal your heart
Because, Mario Luera, I been sprung off you from the start?
Can we sip on some Brandy as I "Put it Down" only for you,
Or would you rather taste Kylie Minogue's "Chocolate" on our rendezvous?

Can I hold you again on the hood of your car like that first night together
As your aroma mixes with mine and clings to my skin, making valuable leather?
Can I give you all the love I have been saving just for "You being you"?
And when I run out of love, will you be down to make some more with all of you?

Chapter IV: Identity in Intimacy

How we define ourselves and how we let others define the sovereign person that we are varies considerably. At times the overall situation is what defines our actions, feelings, and behaviors. In the bedroom the worst of words can be fed to us, but we associate them with pleasure and grow hungry for them. Who we are as lovers differs from how we let others see ourselves under the public eye, only for our borders to be discovered under the private eye. Behind closed doors we let lovers undress us as guards, and walls come down with our clothes. These walls that fall like those at Berlin still succeed in unifying two people: be it momentarily, eternally, or spiritually.

I give you the color red to help set the tone and hue for this chapter, although seemingly cliché red is the most appropriate of the *Colors* to be listed for this chapter of Identity in Shades. In Chinese culture the color red represents happiness and it is often worn during the wedding period, and ceremonies that follow matrimony. Red can also represent sacrifice for in the pursuit of intimacy we sacrifice many resources; be it time or money in order to obtain something greater. The final meaning associated with red that I give to you is that of danger, as to seek intimacy with just anyone can lead to more harm than good. So tread cautiously as you navigate these pieces, enjoy the happiness, understand the sacrifice, and face danger at face value.

Erotica

He writes poetry on her skin with nails dug deep,
And rhythmic words in her mind begin to creep.
He bites down on the sweetness of her mocha skin;
He tempers their love with biblical-proportioned sin.

She sings opera as screams wake neighbors of a possible intruder,
And he lays there hypnotized by her heat, tricked into pursuing her.
She pins him down, spilling out secrets and unknown confessions;
She pulls her belt on him to tame him, branding him with a lesson.

They pour colors of intense varying human creed onto the bedroom floor;
Drill and sculpt their home onto the back of the bathroom door.
She changes faces from shifting positions of intercourse,
And he loses himself inside her until he is no longer more.

We engrave hidden promises onto temporary breathless moments;
We journey paths to the wonderland that is our body seeking fulfillment.
There are no footprints or diseases here, just buckling ankles shaking through fear.
As different shades of color are blended, creating tapestries of us in the wild, fawn and
deer.

Mosaics are created through the differences in height, weight, color, and soul,
But through the breaking down of individual borders, they become whole.
Like two ice sculptures wrapped in each other's embrace, melting into the other's arms,
They continue to stay hot for each other, as though attempting to set off fire alarms.

Imaginar

Imagínate mis dedos tocando te, escuchando a la música que haces.
You are my favorite melody that plays slow jams as we lay.
Imagine the scent of our sweat drip dropping off each other's bodies,
That we soak in each other's essence, delicately, and intimately leaving testimonies.

Te imagino las características de tu cara guapa y en el último momento,
As eyes close then open, and empty hands find me and clinch.
Legs, arms, and insides close, hug, and compress tighter than an Allen wrench;
That for a second we are both lost and found, as we lay together earthbound.

Imagina nos ganado la guerra de amor con dos corazones compartidos
How we'll share and experience more than others and say *"Somos bendecidos."*
Imagine eye lashes heavy with tears of joy that soak us both, absolving our sins.
You don't have to imagine any of this if you just lower your walls, and let me in.
*Imaginar (Spanish for, to imagine)

*Imagínate mis dedos tocando te, escuchando a la música que haces(Spanish for *imagine my fingers touching/playing you, listening to the music you make. Te imagino las características de tu cara guapa y en el ultimo momento (*Spanish for *I imagine the features of your face in that last moment.)Imagina nos ganado la guerra de amor con dos corazones compartidos (*Spanish for *Imagine us winning the war of love with two shared hearts.) Somos bendicidos (*Spanish for, *we are blessed.)*

Memories in the Rain

Cold drops of precipitation soak new clothes that quickly become discarded.

We cling to each other for warmth; soft kisses leave bodies bombarded.

Raindrops, a symphony of sound, digging deeper into your thighs like mounds,

Fertile ground being plowed; your voice rises because I'm endowed.

Foggy glass windows become filled with handprints

Wrestling in an ocean of bed sheets diving deep into waves.

Suffocating, fixating on each other's breath, as sweat trickles down your breast.

Hot air being pushed out from soft lips with each well-intended thrust.

Imprinting upon each other with more than words,

Your nails dig deep into my back, drawing blood.

The sheets become stained with both our blood;

They become a mixture of womanhood and manhood.

Love is a child born betwixt more than two lovers' sheets

Love is that distinct mixture of fear and excitement that makes hearts beat.

Love is lying down with her wrapped under my arms,

Listening to the rain fall, as we both fall slowly into sleep.

Let's Make Music Not Love

Let's make music not love, now you may be curious about this statement;

A question mark that your face has let rise over the aforementioned, the above.

I want to touch your body and strum each cord as we lay,

Do not let the symbolism fool you, this is not play.

Let's make music not love, let us define the colors of the keyboard.

Let the beat be made by the sound of us together.

The rhythm of your hips grinding against mine,

Our bodies making new positions, call that intertwine.

Let's make music not love, as love is temporary feeling that fleets.

Let's create our own rhythm as your head creates beats.

When we both get off our nine to five let's dim the lights and let the world lay quiet.

Let clothes become discarded; let's start six and nine this isn't just it.

Let's make music not love, and if you still have a question mark about the above,

Then let's lay together and listen to the sounds of our hearts beating in sync.

As our headboards become bombarded hiding secret whispers and I love you,

Pictographs of Kama Sutra images placed onto it, as we construct something more.

Let's make love not music, because love can be eternal and music ends with the radio,

So without saying anymore let us hum love songs so we can create our own flow.

Before we decide to stain new and cleaned sheets, let's close our eyes and let minds meet.

Tearstains

Her pillows are bathed and left with tearstains
As male members plunge in her, releasing sex endorphins.
She cries oceans as their bodies make vivid and strong motions.

His face is riddled with tearstains as he pushes harder, exposing veins.
She is his lioness and African queen, her love and womb more valuable than
anything.
He roars thunder, as sheets have been tossed aside so that he may plunder.

Hands grip, tightly occupied with seduction nightly.
If names could ring bells and other things,
Then they were also being engraved upon wedding rings.

Tearstains are beautiful women and handsome men
Grabbing life's reins and roaring wildly like a lion.
Condom slips, explodes the tip, and this is it.

Longing

I cling to your t-shirt as you hold me close,
The scent of your diesel cologne adheres to me.
I want you to touch me, and erase my edges
So you can reach deeper into me.

When you cradle me in your arms and I can,
Hear melodies carried through distant trees.
I want your hands to feel the essence of my soul.
When you're not here I sleep in your T-shirt.
Remembering the love we made...

Remembrance

I bite down on your neck in order to leave a lasting impression
As I instruct you in how pain can be a pleasurable lesson.
I leave a trail of love bites as your body squeezes tight
To warn others that I am the traveler that wanders you at night.

Your toes begin to twitch from immeasurable acts of leisure
Not like a computer glitch, that mimics you only in error.
I whisper to you, "You will remember every bit of this"
As we kiss each other and our tongues tie each other: speechless.

Your soft tone rises into an almost demonic scream
As if awoken in those last few moments of a wet dream.
The light of a shifting sunset is leaking through fine
As you relinquish your name in favor of screaming mine.

I massage love bites with skillful brushstrokes of my tongue
That seem to leave you breathless, as though you were missing a lung.
You will remember this, as my scent clings to you like a fragrance
As your body is left soaking wet with this act of remembrance.

Can You Keep a Secret?

Standing in the hallway on the midnight hour,

Kissing on soft pink lips, your love I'll devour.

My hands unfasten your belt buckle and slip inside,

As you feel the warmth of my palm where your dick hides.

Watching you lick your lips you looked fine,

You got me thinking about six and nine.

I don't know your name or your claim to fame,

Let's just keep quiet and play this dirty game.

Biting on your lips, my hand across your hips.

I'll lay you down quietly, this sensation only last nightly.

You ask me "How hard can you beat it?"

My answer is "Can you keep a secret?"

I'll bind you to your bed,

As you lay there giving me head.

Deep inside I'll go,

Watching your face as you blow.

Giving you more than a bite,

The way you feel inside so tight.

As he lay broken and defeated,

I am resting my fluids depleted.

You drew me close and said

"Daddy you can beat it."

I smile and reply,

"Can you keep a secret?"

Intimate Moon

The promise you made under the silver moonlight

The heavens opened up and brought you to me.

Your eyes like dark pools reflect the white moon.

The stars overhead dance throughout the night sky

A seemingly quiet and pure moment when you held me closer.

Holding me close so surreal and intense, feeling breathless, I black out.

I awaken and cannot help but ask myself, "Was that a dream?"

I turn to you and find that all that had occurred was real.

Fill my heart with song and let me sing forevermore

As I wrap my arms around her, who I began to love.

The first kiss of the morning is both sweet and tender

Your body was heated with passion yet remained calm

Passion that is so out of control and beautiful.

If your eyes were the pure-white moon,

Then my heart would be the tide.

You make my heart rush out of control yet stay so calm.

Your milky-white skin feels so soft against my black palm.

As I press myself against you for the second time

And I whisper "no blacking out this time" as we rest

And you seduce me within the radiant brilliance of the night.

Sweetness

She bathes her body in lavender bath salts

As *su cuerpo tiembla** and her fingers wash away bits of asphalt.

Her caramel sweetness soaks in the tub as she begins to clean,

Letting the lavender solution wash away Hershey's Kisses as though a dream.

She awakens to fields painted with a Skittles rainbow and blank canvas to paint with.

She swallows her sugar daddy's morsels and sweetness, regardless of length or width.

She scrubs delicate ankles with a fresh and unworn loofah

And unwinds herself carefully until she falls into a stupor.

Her fingernails tell tales of light rails and holding onto Red Vines,

They broke from her being pressed and losing herself when he calls her "mine."

Her buttercup ears know the sounds of cool and calming pillow talk;

Hear the sounds of escalating voices as she climbed Jack's beanstalk.

*Su cuerpo tiembla is Spanish for "her body trembles."

Nightmare

In the silence of the night with darkness hiding all that there was, it crept in.

With haste it came into my room and quickly hid itself under the covers I slept in.

Not yet quite awake but fully erect, I felt the fear of something unknown as I slept.

Fingers bathed in the mystery of a room void of light, and it takes me: a grand theft.

Tossing, turning, screaming, and burning as fear and excitement shake me

In a half-attempt for this foreign nightmare to awaken me.

The shadows that slumbered at the foot of my bed have begun to stand in audience.

The terror of the nightmare transforms itself into pure forbidden decadence.

As voices rise and eyes once shut now gaze deep into that lost midnight heat,

And bodies make motions and consume one another; as eyes shut and flutter on repeat.

Tossing, turning, screaming, and burning as fear and excitement shake me

In a half-attempt for this foreign nightmare to awaken me.

In the quietness of the night with darkness enveloping all that there was, you crept in.

With haste you came into my room and quickly hid within the covers we slept in.

Not yet quite awake but fully erect, I felt the horror of not knowing where I slept.

Fingers bathed in the mystery of a room void of light, and you steal me away: theft!

Your Hands

Quietness crept into my bed as you often did;
Its fingertips ran up my spine as if tracing me,
Making an outline of my body and soul.

I turn over to see your undisturbed resting place,
Letting myself unravel silently until you return.
Waiting still for you to come close and draw me in
To put contents into my container and make love with the remainder.

On quiet evenings you'd lie awake waiting for my spirit to unwind
As though waiting to find a piece of yourself within me to define.
You let yourself unfold and release your heartstrings to connect to mine.

We create tapestries in the dark as hands not able to see each other:
Pull, rip, cut, and sew new works that are made in the absence of light.
Just for our eyes to witness these works in morning glory, not moonlight.

Warmth crept gently into my bed like you often did;
Its soft lips planted kisses on me as if expecting me to melt,
Then your hands take hold of me and remold me in that kiln called my room.

I Wanna

"Baby close your eyes and just listen."
I wanna hear you scream "Oh My God"… at the altar,
Before you waver and let your precious chastity falter.
I wanna get your lips soaking wet… as they drip with wine,
Rather than exploit your self-lubricating features, before I make both lips mine.

I wanna see how well you ride… with me on a trip,
Well before I see how well you ride and handle the tip.
I wanna undress your… yes I wanna undress your heart,
Rather than have you discard what you are wearing from the start.

I wanna be deep inside of you…to a place many haven't been to, your soul.
Before I contemplate how we connect our private members to make us both
whole.
I wanna make you come… yes come let us spend some of your time together.
Long before I watch your body tightens up and release, as you handle my flesh
tether.

I wanna watch your body pulsate and shine… in its own luminescence,
Before you lower humble yourself to your knees as though seeking repentance.
I wanna show you that this is far from celibacy, that this is a commitment.
Like that of a contractor who is willing to lay down his pipe into the cement.

I wanna explore the vast crevasses of your skin, to find in you in women,
To create art with it as we lower our boundaries, and let the other one in.
I wanna let you know that I love to eat out…Japanese,
But I'd rather cook for you before we both rely on our knees.

"Baby open your eyes and you can see,
That all these metaphors, moments, and love are coming from me.

I wanna romance you… to forget about the sunrise and enjoy this view,

Baby your kisses are sunshine, and they give me morning wood to look forward

to."

Colors

He and I express lovemaking not in actions but diverse colors and hues.

We finger paint our souls with colors of the rainbows well past curfews.

We let white bedsheets become our blank canvases,

Even after headboards break and we repair the damages.

He and I are royal shades of purple and indigo like that of a king.

I wear him like a crown before I wear him down and hear him sing.

We transform my lap into a throne so he can rest

As we let shades of violet turn cardinal like those of a blood test.

He and I are passionate shades of red and crimson;

We use protection so that no unknown illness leads to treason.

We transform cold whispers into hot screams for the neighbors to hear.

As we heat up and cool down, we let our shades condense into a crystal blue tear.

He and I are shades of deep and haunting colors of sapphire blue.

Constantly diving deeper into each other, finding new places to test our virtue.

We transform tears of sorrow into beautifully wept tears of joy

As green youth create lush moments in the depth of boy on boy.

He and I are shades of bright and youthful pigments of green,

Both resisting and succumbing to hormones, wanting to "get in between."

We transform salty flavor into pineapple-juice-sweetened *lecheros*.

As we come and rise, both come and rise into shades of yellow.

He and I are golden sunsets and sunrises fundamentally yellow.

We greet each other with warm hugs and cold kisses as we relinquish "Hello."

We transform shiny golden foil magnum wrappers into trash can covers.

As they are used and filled up, we remain whole and paint ourselves orange lovers.

He and I are shades of sweet tangerines and juicy oranges.

We barricade ourselves within the world we call "us" and bolt down door hinges.

We transform ourselves with nectarine-flavored kisses and fruitful labor.

As we plow each other's fertile fields without need of a hoe, as we are together.

Coffee (Black Women)

To me, black women are like coffee.

They are harvested on African and Brazilian shores.

They can turn men neurotic with their mocha narcotic.

They are morning warmth and scolding tongues.

Black women at a certain age become processed by many unappreciative men.

They become bitter yet refined like a warm cup of black coffee on a cold day.

Although black women come in different flavors and hues,

Like coffee, if you are sweet to them, they will keep you up past curfews.

To me, black women are like coffee.

Handle them firm yet tenderly, or become scolded.

They can keep you up, like Folgers in your cup.

So please pour me another refill of a black woman in my cup.

Seduction (Biopsych)

As I began to stimulate her afferent nerves

And my smooth muscles become erect from her curves,

I want to be dopamine, and she can be my serotonin

As hearts stop receiving acetylcholine and produce norepinephrine.

She gives my parasympathetic system something to rest and digest

As I swim helplessly like an animal inside her learned helplessness test.

My positive energy has me connecting my axon to her voltage gate

As she receives these sexual neurotransmitters at her chemical gate.

I look forward to seeing how her anxiety handles my open-arm test

As I feed her something she craves deep in her hypothalamus.

I want to stimulate her amygdala and her PNS

As sensory and motor neurons interact; CNS.

They say you can't have your cake and eat it.

I wouldn't mind having a sagittal cut of her cake and eat it.

I want to trigger her EPSP and watch as she performs exocytosis

As I release myself, and she cleans up the remainder with pinocytosis.

Chapter V: Identity in Understanding Self

I present to you this final chapter of poetic work, though it is not the final chapter within this book. The poems, like all previous sections, are 100 percent authentic within themselves and the sentiment that was used to create them. These poems consist of bits of slam poetry and of poems that may not be at all relative to anyone else but me. At first glance, some of these verses may seem similar to the first section of the book; however, I must assure you that, unlike the previous section, this section focuses on the power and perspective of the individual's effect on society, whereas the aforementioned section focuses on how the group, community, and society influence the perspectives and lives of the individual.

I ask that you tread lightly and walk circumspectly as you enter the final stage, which may ask you to reexamine yourself and even me. When examining ourselves, at times we lack a certain honesty that the outside world may view us as. At times the only way we see ourselves is by judging others by projecting images and traits that we dislike in ourselves onto others. By doing this act, by committing this attribution, we find catharsis and relief. Once you have projected these things onto my poetry, onto me, or onto those strange faces in the hallway, I recommend that you take it one step further and ask yourself why. Now you needn't outwardly ask or tell anyone the answer to this question, but I do highly recommend that you do indeed ask it. For in answering this question, you will learn the nature of prejudice and love to an extent—as we both love and hate ourselves—and how we perceive others is a reflection of our own internal equilibrium.

The color that I associate this chapter and its associated meanings with is green. The color green can represent youth, hope, the environment, and health. I am within this youthful spectrum of sorts, being only twenty-three at the moment that I have written this collective work, but I must further astound you by informing you that some of this included work was written at the age of fifteen.

Hope is something that we all need in order to carry ourselves through the day and to help alleviate the stressors and problems that could kill us. The following poems also reflect my spiritual, mental, and physical health in relation to the environment.

I Speak Verses

My words, which carry bits of intellectual property, are not my own.
They're secrets, gospels, songs, and languages taken from us by the English throne.
I have unearthed these tall tales and kernels of truth for which the world shall atone.
I stand at my mic tall and proud, standing on the backs of those who have come before me.

Not fearing the possibility of actions forged of hate or by those who claim to adore me,
I have spoken both ill and great things, so I lack a God complex, self-appointed holy.
My voice, which travels from caverns for which I hid it for fear of others' persecution,
Has now become quick to ignite the mic and begin this execution.

The sounds created from my tongue are both deep in tone and soft in delivery.
They mirror my actions deep and rich in meaning unafraid of implanting a memory.
I am Spanish speaking, Choctaw chanting, Japanese singing sound that won't stop
But quickly retreats into its cavern at the sound of an omnidirectional gun pop!

Disclaimer!

Warning: the words that this pen writes,
Which are repeated as the sound of my keys type, will paint images in your head.
This may invoke a sensation of dread.
Take a grain of salt with that, and in the morning, let it be reread.

Drowsiness is not a side effect of my poetry or flow,
But you may face some growing pains you never wanted to know.
Face messages subliminal, breaking into your mind's eye, criminal.

Planting ideas in your mind: inception, birth of new thoughts, conception.
I'll change your dosage from free verse to sonnets.
Nurse you on my bosom like children, bonnets.

These words may seem lethal, killing both ignorance and ignorant people.
I am your medicine man and doctor, the one in front of the crowd: proctor.
This is my warning, an open disclaimer like a classic whipping from a lion tamer.
Take one dose daily and rejoice in the act, inebriation like Bailey, hops.

Criminal words that invoke running from a higher authority, cops.
Language is my cage from which I release my rage.
I am not a cardiologist, but this will affect your heart.
I am not a psychologist, but I will affect your mental condition.
I am not a painter, but these images will stain those windows called perception.

Spoken Truth

This is potent poetry through sincerity,
Spoken truth that is more than literary.
Let me prove this with point in delivery,
So strong that it is deadly even in reverie.

Are we as a people lobotomized by a twin-sided needle
Of materialism and greed, becoming shallow like a puddle?
When did America become a business and not a country?
Measuring our self-worth with stock-market currency.

It is delicacy delivered through spoken elegancy
That inflicts injury, shortening life expectancy.
Take care of this poetic being like a pregnancy;
Make your body a home for it, humble residency.

Greed

I seek not monetary value to feed my every need,
Feeding people and that hungry monster called greed.
It is through growing up on hard times and poverty
That my family fed me life lessons of modesty.

I don't brag at the fact that at times my pockets are a presidential cemetery
Or yell out ignorance magnified louder through microphones by rap; immorality.
I am not someone obsessed over the value of trivial things.
Rather drown myself in the brave voices of Gandhi and Dr. King.

I'm Black and American Indian and a walking tree,
So I'm well rooted in ancestral foundations out of necessity.
Unlike thirsty rappers who speak of making it rain in order to quench their pain,
I am fed on cultural indigenous dances that make Mother Nature wet and rain.

As my vintage Jordans push the gas pedal down on my '88 Benz,
Like my car, time and money are best invested internally, not on rims.
Choosing not to live lavishly and managing money affordably
So that I'm not like fools who, much like their cars, stay on E.

Zombies

People claim in false glory to be king of the hill
But seldom realize like Tyree they're on my heel;
Achilles seemingly focused on perfection and not his weakness.
A lesson most unlearned; let me redirect my emphasis.

People become hungry with unquenchable lust for items; zombies.
Sedating themselves from beautiful scenery, getting higher than palm trees.
Representing man's fear of the undying need to kill our resources,
Like darkness, living monsters derived from imaginary sources.

I am not a medic; I am a cleric,
Preaching work from God; at times they deem odd.
Teens have materialistic ideals, leave homes empty, silent hill.
While gangsters and cops gun each other down, resident evil.

Tea Leaves

I spoke to a friend and asked him, "How is your heart?"
He replied, "It's cold and bitter from being played."
I responded, "My heart is bitter and hot."
Much to his amusement and my own he asked, "Why?"

"My heart is bitter and hot like fresh black tea.
It gives warmth and comfort to visitors on the nightly.
Inside the bitter taste are lessons of patience not to haste,
To enjoy my sweetness, and savor this taste."

The remnants of who I am in present day
Are tea leaves waiting to be used again one day.
To comfort the sick and ill, to relieve stuffiness,
To create heartfelt moments at that first kiss.

What it Means to Write

What it means to write is to give these feelings home
When thoughts turn into emotion left wild to roam.
What it means to write is to clearly define moments
That leave me speechless, encoding feelings of remembrance.

But what is the significance of these scribbles?
When the amount of happiness-derived words I drop are just mere ripples?

What it means to write is to have something to hold on to at night.
It creates rhythm, harmonies, prose, and song if the melody is right.
What it means to write is that with the foundation of emotion to cry,
I give my pen richness of life and remove the fear that it should die.

But what does an undying pen do for me
Except draw thin dotted lines between brilliance and insanity?

What it means to write is to give record to an instant
Like a ghost trapped in time, repeating its action, a poetic remnant.
What it means to write is to give strength, solidarity, and wisdom,
All for the convenience of many a reader at one mere stroke of my pen.

The Promise of Glitter

I am a moment of intense desire trapped in limbs, covered in the devil's flesh.
I am intense longing for the envelopment that leaves anxiety-driven hearts restless.
My skin is a Black, Red, and Brown road map that shows lovers' handprints and sin.
Hands play bodily chords; escalating voices harmonize into a degrading hymn.

Like glitter I shine brightly, not in stationary or concentrated form
But only while falling or on some stranger's interest I adorn.

I am half-open eyes seeking to let go of melancholy, to be undressed by a foreigner.
My body is a land that has been visited by travelers with no returning caller.
My soul bathes deep in Christian morality but finds lack of warmth in divinity.
My pelvis grinds like an herbal wheel for carelessness in need to cure an STD.

Like glitter I shine defiantly against the norm
But am subjected to black projected images of porn.

Strong legs, which run three-mile laps in 23:15, and an 8.5-length dick hangs in between.
It waits not to be seen but to be exposed to a new, unknown scene.
One that paints the skies full of beautiful mango-colored sunrise,
Not one of wanderers' eyes seeking to find what lies in between my thighs.

Like glitter I shine brightly as I am brushed off
With yesterday's deeds being embroidered on me in scarlet-red cloth.

I am self-respecting hands and long, delicate black fingertips.
Those are undressed and unraveled by an unknown grip.
I am words of warning and awareness that I am sin incarnate;
I am the passion and desperation embroidered in the letter scarlet.

I am addicted to excitement and fear of not knowing who comes next;
I am glitter that lay downtrodden and useless after sex.

Good-Bye

I lay restlessly dreaming in the allotment of time between a stare and a blink.
My strength is turning into weakness as I lay too tired to contemplate or think.
Wishes and dreams float before my shallow yet deep, starring eyes
As tears erupt, overflow, and wash away all the truths and all the lies.

As my presence and health fade, I exchange a sigh for a memory with you.
Fingers too weak to hold on to the present must now bid the future farewell too.
If I am to fade into nothing but the sweetness of a memory, remember me.

A weakened heart beats, skips, runs, and falls within a small distance that I must walk.
Half a lung gone, and I fall breathless like the Giant from the bean stalk.
I am human for the moment, made equal before that kind being called death;
I am desperate reverie wishing to share with you one last, loving breath.

As my aroma is swept away into yesterday's driveway, I am filled with longing,
Remembering how I never stood on sturdy ground, so I kept on falling.
If I am to fade into nothing but the name you recall, know "That for you I fall."

As my thick hair thins, my straight back bends, and limbs grow beat-up and weary,
Know that you never held me down, but I wish once more you'd hold me dearly.
I am God for the moment, seeing both life and death;
I am the Devil's anger over the boy you left.

As my footprints disappear, a reminder that I was here, I rhyme to myself.
"Did you hear, did you hear, the boy who hid his fear at the unsightly rumor?
Well I bet you didn't know what weighed him down was a heart-thriving tumor!"

I recline effortless in between the time afforded between anger and bitterness.
I lay still for hours due to lack of vital energy not college-kid laziness. I have made my
peace with this, and On your presence I shall reminisce.
As tears erupt, overflow, and wash away all the half-truths and white lies,
I lay sleeping now from a cancerous lullaby.

Name

My name translates into *God's Flint*,

A stone that ignites light and heat for others.
A flint is a stone that has neither of these substances,
Yet it comforts those in need of them.

This stone was used to build Solomon's temple.
This stone, whose name I share, that I build with.
A temple is a sturdy foundation of hard work;
It boasts knowledge and tall structure made by the masses.

I am both of these things in reality and metaphor.
I give warmth and that light called hope to the needy
Even if I lack both of these to keep for myself;
I am a large structure holding both wisdom and community.

Unsung Lullabies

Your hands and feet were erased before you could crawl
By a unilateral decision when you were three weeks small.
I sing for you in my melancholy this lullaby,
One that will never soothe your needy cry.

I will never know the anguish of your terrible two's
Or comfort you from teenage-romance blues.
Your unheard heartbeat will be sorely missed,
Yet it was erased by the women I had kissed.

Save Me

I am so tired of praying and yelling at my cross,
Hoping some figure will find me because I'm so lost.
Some divine father figure will come off his throne
And lead me to a better place, yet I stand here alone.

I need this feeling, this heavy-weighing doubt, off my chest,
So I can rest assured there is righteous love when I say, "God bless."
I don't want to sound improper in any way, but this is what I feel.
Time and time again it seems I'd gain more relief from a pill
Than to pray and hope that God's grace and mercy are real.

Yes I am filled with doubt and have learned not to walk so blindly,
But not once has that stopped me from living Christian morals and acting kindly.
To me God is love; to them my love is wrong; but how could I know what love is
When I have seen violent things done in its name, leaving me a traumatized witness?
I need someone tangible to help save me, to show me that this sorrow isn't just me.
Dealing with this storm inside of me is pushing me down the road to insanity.

Israel once said to me with unwavering pride in his Christianity that I am a fighter.
However, I am a man who has been knocked down just trying to go higher.
I know that I stand now as some amazing symbol, some Lifetime/Disney movie
On a kid raised by a single mom struggled and made his name out of poverty,
But I am here to reinforce the fact that I am not a hero; I am left with self-esteem zero,
Which leaves me contemplating horrible things like King Nero, as I sing, "*Me muero.*"*

Like words from female rapper Nicki Minaj, I ask that you please "Save me,"
But I've given up on a savior who will come through and rescue me.
Like before I move forward on shaking and unsettling ground taking the next step,
Unsure of when I will be allowed to rest and shown love, not designated a pest.

The weak have it good as they have each other to rely on
While I have only myself for whose shoulder I can cry on.
They say, "Stand your ground, and place your feet where you see fit."
But as I look around me, no one is there, and I am left to stand in this shit.

*Me muero is Spanish for *I'm dying.*

Psychology

Am I as a man a sum of his emotions, or a diagnosis of Major Depression?
Am I a fool whose obsession over negativity affected my cognition?
Was it sparked in childhood for lack of self-efficacy?
Or is my mental state just a product of self-fulfilling prophecy?

Is it to blame on the heads of founders Freud, Sigleman, and Pearson?
Are my behaviors correlative to my association with major depression?
Or would humanists say its cause is the environment, this recession?
Do I suffer labels from abnormal psychology for forensic psych to judge me?

Would the biologist argue that it was a chemical imbalance they could cure?
Was it the psychoanalyst theory that I'd had too many failed attempts to procure?
Are these feelings inherited partially due to Piaget and his theory?
Can I be freed from it by flooding or by building a fear hierarchy?

I know not the cause of such emotional constancy,
Be its roots in psychology or unspoken divinity.
Within these thoughts I have found a name to say,
To label these feelings, and it's called *Wednesday!*

Cognitive Psychology

Forgive me if your first impression becomes deluded by a reverie
As past episodic memories found through rich encoding do remind me.
Will not allow you into my life without first bringing up my long-term memory.
Now I have decided to give you my utmost focus in selective attention
Even though you were dichotic, listening to other male voices I didn't mention.

Now you act as if you don't recognize my face, symptoms of agnosia.
But you leave me speechless Broca's and Wernicke's aphasia.
I just hope Noam Chomsky was right, and the language of love is an innate ability.
That even if I do learn it late for my age that I can still obtain fluency,
And I truly hope that we can operationalize love and not rely on semantic memory.

My Eulogy

If I am your most painful memory,
In moments of significant pain, remember me.
For it's I who hurt you and drew you near.
Spoken words like daggers at you, my dear; don't fear.

If I am your most loving memory,
When you are lonely, hold my memory in your heart and cradle me.
For in catching secondary glances, be it friendship or romances,
We stumbled upon something cosmic and have taken these chances.

If I am your most hilarious and comedic memory,
When you need a feeling of joy, remember me.
So when you're making first impressions
You use my jokes to avoid negative transgressions.

If I am your favorite memory,
Then please try and remember me.
Because remembrance is love,
And in that, I loved you consistently.

Exodus

The garden from which I awoke lay cold and dissolute.
Once heavily flowered by friends and family, it lay barren.
That first breath in solitary leaves a bittersweet taste.
I push forward into the wilderness, my shadow holding my hand.

This is my exodus, the Eden I had long since forgotten and held on to
Lay tenderly cradled in those who placed these seeds for success.

Across the vast terrain, an unfamiliar silhouette smiles at me.
I walk this distance among a forest of people, none of whom can hear me.
I sit now in a town where no one knows my name and relieve myself of it.
This cold city none of my family or friends have known calls to me.

This is my exodus, the Eden I had long since let go of from these hands
Lay trapped in that last tear I held as I faced the morning star ahead.

I rest my head in a room that is mine only in name and disappear into a reverie.
Where the taste of mom's cooking, the hot summer breeze, and ice-cream bells
All have been preserved perfectly in my memory.
This place where friendships do not die,
And we grow stronger and see through every ominous lie.

This is my exodus, the Eden I had left behind that day
Lay forever etched into my memory.

I walk amid a world, which knows not of this self-imposed exodus,
Knowing that I cannot return to that Eden I left undefiled by the world.
I take this knowledge of the world that I was given by chance
And stand naked in front of the world I must now face.

Vocal

I spoke in a voice that was not quite a whisper,
Removed cotton from a bottle of pills labeled *Don't take with liquor.*
Eight pills poured out of the bottle like Skittles into children's hands.
I shuffled them around with a crooked finger; mother's contraband.

Yes medicine can become poison; it heals infections and nulls unbearable pain.
Inscribes in us life lessons but, indulging, rids us of life's strain.
I am an old spirit in a young body with knowledge beyond my age.
My voice lay silent now, something you can't find on any octave.

Dots (Pointillism)

Every horrible thing that happens is for a reason.
It's like thousands of seemingly insignificant dots:
Though they may seem useless at the time
They make a beautiful image in the end.
Even if you're the only one that can see it.

However, if you blind yourself with pain and sorrow,
Those dots may appear as a hole deep inside of your soul,
At the very core of your existence, void of compliments.
And if that hole continues to grow, it will devour you,
So connect the dots and find a deeper meaning.

Don't say stupid things like, "I hate people," or "I can't love."
In time those dots will make a path leading you to happiness.
So let the light that is hope shine pure in your eyes.

In time wounds will heal, and tears will dry.
Open your eyes and see all the vibrant colors.
Connect the dots!

Just Thr33 Lozers

I rode my bike as the world lay silent and crept along the sidewalk,
Breaking blades of grass as I peddled forward.
Gliding through the east-blowing winds,
I raise my arms from the handle bars,
And I pretend to fly.

I pass my favorite corner store,
And I can hear the sounds of yesterday
Completely ambush me with the nostalgia of summer.
The smell of orange trees as I lose myself in a reverie
Of those days when I lay shy.

I make my way to a house once shrouded in colorful glow.
Roses that climbed up the walls of so many vast colors
Have all been cut down, and the place where we sat
Shaded by the roof and fueled by Little Caesar's
Has grown quiet in our absence.

Just a little farther, and I flew by our old hangout,
And light shone brightly onto that spot
As if the sun was pouring out its entire splendor.
I opened my eyes with full clarity at our bonds
As if I was born again in that light, and I saw
The world as if I had opened my eyes for the first time.

Now I am home, and my bike takes its rest.
I have no memories of the three of us here,
Only the hopes and anxious, choking feeling.
Praying for the next day to come sooner,
For the light of dawn to break through early,
So that I might see you again, my friends.

Homecoming

I arrive home to one-hundred-degree weather and to the comfort of a cold lolicup.
To homicide sirens, graffiti walls signifying caution to look around and not up.
The quietness of my room is filled with the sound of seldom-heard ringtones
As a multitude of the friends contact me to set up kick-it dates via phone.

I am fed on Chinese food by John Garcia, on Taco Bell with my homie Israel Moran.
I run into friends like Eric Guerro, talk with Adeel over a Saturday-lunch plan.
I return to find whole families relocated and neighborhood unity no longer present.
I find death on my street caused by inner-city entrapment and gang resentment.

I am rooted in family-owned businesses and restaurants that exist here no more.
As unique places filled with comfort like Aranda's becomes a Dollar General Store.
For a moment, I find myself a stranger to this city that I had to learn to call home,
But home is not a place; it's a time and destination where my friends meet and roam.

I'm Tired (Compliments)

I am tired, beaten, and worn down within moments of new greetings.
I let loose sincerity, trust, and good loving in daily meetings,
And therein lies the problem, as they cannot see the distance it must travel.
They lack the perspective that all these things are precious gifts, which I must unravel.

My enduring and gregarious actions are built up on strong arms
That kept being pushed away, scolded, and screaming: fire alarms.
These hands that are both soft to touch but cracked
Bring more than abundance of deed, but reveal a difficult road map.

They crossed rivers of tears without comfort or reassurance,
Through echoing mountains of dull and played-out compliments.
I find neither warmth nor relief of pain in the fickle attraction to my frame.
When they become so quickly enamored and protest love yet know not my name.

I am tired, beaten, and worn down from empty promises that you might stick around,
And although I play as a post in basketball, I refuse to be your rebound.
So do me a favor and do it moving because everything you're about is a joke to me.
They lack the perspective to see that their games are played out like Atari.

Dances with Clouds

I am the wind that tickles at a stranger's neck,
The voice in the sky that pushes out "Good-bye" with no regret.
I am size-eighteen moccasins dancing at the Bakersfield Standing Bear Powwow,
The rhythm of the earth beating on the drum telling us, "It's time to dance now."

We are Smiling Fox, Shadow Hawk, and Golden Bear, indigenous names aplenty.
We are varying feet scurrying around trying not to be late to Grand Entry.

I am the mother mound of the Choctaw people,
Of Creek and Blackfoot but still Black to most people.
We are stomachs hungry for fry bread or the expensive Indian taco.
We are of varying lower economic families, hoping to win the Lotto.

I am American English, Cuban Spanish, Chatah Anumpa, and Ojibwa,
The current heir to a history of bloodlines presented in front of you today.
I am black regalia, pink, and silver ribbons made by Mary, doing a grass dance.
I am the living ghost here and alive miraculously, not by mere chance.

Kappa Sigma

I am a Kappa Sigma a member of a gentleman's society,
Taking pride in our brotherhood, not a frat but a fraternity.
We are fellowship, service, leadership, diligence, and community unity.
Bounded by oaths under silence and secrecy we say, "AEKDB."

I am rho class at this Omicron Mu chapter.
We create our own life stories, redefining *happily ever after*.
Yes we are Kappa Sigma, easily spotted and recognized.
We boast high GPAs, community service, and parties of large size.

We are walking the halls at CSU Bakersfield with fraternal rivals in DZT
But need only make reference to this year's Greek-week defeat eloquently.
We are a variety of creeds with depth and richness in cultural colors
But honor our differences and call ourselves brothers.

We are acting foolishly at Dance Marathon, seeking money to procure,
Fighting together strongly bonded at Relay for Life, raising funds for a cure.
We are secret handshakes and words others wish to replicate and configure,
Moving into our own places and becoming public and historical figures.

Moving Day

The alarm clock rings loudly in place of my neighbor's rooster,
Reminding me it's eight o'clock, and I must get ready to move.
I jump into a shower that is not quite hot yet and surrender to it.
I let my thick black hair that nature curls into thick beads moisten
As head and shoulders unravel them, and I let thoughts soak in.

I still have many things left unpacked, such as toothbrushes, socks, and my body wash.
I stumble onto a wet floor with last-minute anxiety, unable to find my packed cloth.
I sift through prepackaged clothes in attempt to find myself today's outfit.
"Not blue or black jeans; no, not ankle socks; does this shirt still fit?"

I am dressed from head to toe in my own style mixed with urban décor.
I scramble impatiently in last-ditch attempts to finish packing my car.
The oil, brakes, and tires have been replaced, making sure that they don't waste.
I lift up grandmother's and great-grandmother's pans delicately, not with haste.

I fill my stomach on yesterday's rice with fresh chorizo on an eighty-year-old pan.
I make sure that I wash and oil them in the traditional manner by hand.
I fill blank CDs with songs of my ancestral culture and those of pop culture,
Close my bedroom door one last time, and bid good-bye as I make my departure.

My little green car that I squish both myself and my things in
Begins to start itself as I release the brake and put key to ignition.
I drive away with Stockton in my rearview mirror and a future ahead of me
As I bob and weave between diesel trucks and new Mustangs.
This is my moving day, sentiment pushing forward like a train.

Believe

The value of light is not appreciated until we are lost in a curtain of darkness,
When our limbs are weary, and the mind has lost itself and become senseless.
"I have lost something so important over something so small," Utada Hikaru,
And though mine is not love based it's not something I can push through.

I have let my "Whispers of the Moon" grow silent and lose my "Memories in the Rain."
When I am reminded of what I can no longer do and become riddled with pain.
I lost my grip and fell out of my place, stumbled hard, and landed on my face.
I became *yami*, the Japanese word for *darkness*, my expression of hopelessness.

My disappearing voice called out, and though faint, it was help I did find.
I received encouragement from brothers like Nathan Campbell, a.k.a. Blue.
Found arms to help me up through the DeCamron Foundation and others to turn to.

I had let myself relinquish all forms of hope, only to be filled with thoughts of suicide.
These many thoughts were truly bugging, and they brought the pesticide.
There were alumni who came to my aid, faceless, constructing a support enclave.

I became *hikari*, the Japanese word for *light*, the ability to stand up, to fight.
Thank you, brother Doug, Mr. Russo, Sam, Zandre, Joshua, and Nate for your stories.
Thanks to Showers of Blessing and Garden Community for your supportive ministries.
"The best part of believe is the lie," Fallout Boy.
We live in a world of contradictions, and I'm glad that you all are the truth.

Mother

Growing up, I heard my mom speak in two languages: recipe and scripture.
I didn't understand everything, yet I knew she carried them proudly with her.
I was nursed on the bosom of a six-foot-tall Black and Native American woman.
She is strong in virtue though her bones are weak, and in that she built our home in.

Mother's hands are shiny, wrinkled road maps bathed in blessing oil.
They are brown turf packed on red clay to create fertile soil.
She is early morning Sunday Service, midday salsa, and evening *Law and Order*.
She is judge, jury, and prosecutor of our oversized household and keeper of order.

Mom is a teacher in Psalms, Proverbs, the Old Testament, and those of Dr. Seuss.
She suffers from body pain that medication can't remedy and sees a masseuse.
She is supporting mother, loving grandmother, and knowledgeable great-grandmother.
She is a fountain of wisdom that freely gives aid so that others won't suffer.

Mom spent time in both Oakland and great-grandmother's land in Colusa,
Ignored lessons in herbs and tribal language but still had hard stares; Medusa.
She juggled two jobs, a day commute, and volunteered at Shepherd's Gate.
She spoke words of blessing, advocacy, and of preparedness as not to show up late.

Father the Provider

When I was younger and all the strength that was in the world
Was absolutely stitched into the fibers of all the muscles in my dad's arms,
I would sit as if on top of the world but in reality on the top of my father's shoulders.
My father smelled of beer, a morning jog's sweat, and of the Bay Area breeze.
His hair was like black pepper with grains of salt mixed in.

In childhood, Dad didn't have money to spend on buying my nephew and I clothes,
But he could afford trips to the Bay Area and the Whoppers that filled our stomachs.
Though he worked few hours, he paid us both allowances equivalent to our age.
The three of us spent time picking berries at Diamond Oak Park,
Only to return to the comforts of his apartment and mix them into sherbet.

In the time of adolescence, in which both my age and allowance had grown,
He provided support by appearing at chess tournaments and school meetings.
Though not always eager, he was always willing to provide a ride to play Yu-gi-oh.
He spent money on family trips to Vegas and meager shopping sprees.
He bought a new TV and leather couches in an attempt to turn a house into a home.

In the time of my teenage years, I was provided with rides to the mental facility.
There I was sedated with antidepressants and appointments with a therapist.
He provided me with anger to use in order to succeed from his words and actions.
He gave away commodities, like my first car, and frustrating driving lessons.
He provided a ticket to spend time with family in Mexico; no home, so I had to go.

In the time of my adulthood, all the strength I needed was now on my shoulders.
I enrolled in college and there he gave me a car to travel with and gospel to learn.
He had no funds or time to spend but gave words of encouragement
As time ages us both, and we try to lower the borders set up by resentment.

Choctaw Rey (Ode to Rap)

A lot of mainstream rappers spit rhymes hypocritical,
Leaving underground rappers and urban poets to kill them: lyrical.
Their dead careers can't be measured by instruments empirical
While urban poets ready their verses and pens ready to kill.

They once went hard like a rock, steady in their foundation,
Only to be eroded by mainstream waters; degradation.
They turn their lives and lives of others into a commodity for pop acculturation,
Heads held high, embracing false images of 'hoods and lifestyles in humiliation.

We glorify the lifestyle of 10 percent of the American population,
Then sell it like 1930s gangster films, leading to moral pollution.
Now don't get it twisted; I respect a lot of those out there fighting for their families,
But I have no love or respect for those who stay sedated, spending money on drugs not
Huggies.

How can you objectify women one moment and in the next say you *love* her?
When you spit rhymes that demean her and all those who came before her?
As her mom is fed on stories of slave auctions passed down from great-grandmother,
Of how her own sisters were turned into commodities, and sold off in front of her.

Now this may lead to negative feedback aimed at me, Choctaw Rey,
As they try to find weakness in me, liking both, erroneously label me gay.
Let me take a moment to educate all of you to what it means when you sag,
As it was invented by men hungry to be fucked by men in prison, so who is the fag?

Closet Doors

A boy at the age of fourteen was the emotional victim of a horrific scene.
One that was birthed from telling his mother and father that he was in between.
He was shaky size-fourteen boots in the ninth grade at Franklin High.
He was called into the principal's office due to confusion, which ended in, "I'm bi."

A boy at the age of fourteen who never really hid in the closet
Now lived in war, as with giving honesty his peace he had to forfeit.
He was sweaty hands on the hour bus ride home, soaked in anxiety.
He was met by silence and nothing else as he entered his residency.

A boy at the age of fourteen who was already living on unstable ground
Wanted support and courage, but it was only disapproval and shame he found.
He was self-loathing Christian and an abomination, a sodomite.
He was hiding tears, fear, and bruises in his pillows at night.

A boy at the age of fourteen hoped and prayed that mother's love he'd redeem.
Upon disclosure, she was quiet and tearful; he lived in a nightmare not a dream.
He was so far over the edge and deeply afraid of feeling more rejection
As he killed himself by attending antigay Sunday school lessons.

A boy at the age of fourteen grew into a man at twenty one.
One who had faced fights, homophobic teammates, and more to come.
He was homeless six times at his father's prideful hands.
He was emotionally hollow from mother's Christian demands.

A boy at the age of fourteen was brutally murdered on that coming-out day.
When he told his parents that he was *bisexual* and they heard *gay*.
He was emotionally, spiritually, and psychologically damaged by this history,
How those who were supposed to love him turned him into a horror story.

God

I find myself trying to understand this complex relationship I have with God.
My body is a temple, and my heart is the window through which all must enter.
Though my foundation in the church has brought me this far, it is my mind that…

To some, God is the omnipresent father.
To them, God is authoritative, absolute, strong, destructive, and constructive.
He creates obstacles that punish the righteous and the wicked.
God is both strict and distant to his children even when they are at the altar.

To some, God is seen as a brother.
To them, God is a familiar and distinct companion that they traverse with.
He is a member of their family and glorifies it with sanctity of marriage.
God is both fellowship and kinship, which makes him easy to obtain.

To some, God is seen as a lover.
To them, God hits an unknown spot that is unreachable to any other.
He gives words that are sweet and supple like breasts to nurse mankind.
God is abundance of intimacy that outside of his kingdom you can't find.

I am not entirely sure of where to put the check mark of us in any category.
So I simply open my heart to let God know he has a place to dwell in.
He creates warm kisses on cold days and somber melodies of love.
God is warm, undying, honest, nurturing love, so I give glory to him above.

Choctaw

Dear *Isht Chito*, I am a descendant of your people.
My grandmother, who was born from your womb,
Accidentally traveled west to *Atuklant Illi* for a future;
And here she laid down her children who didn't know your name.

Dear *Chitokaka*, I am a descendant of your people.
I am a *shilup* seeking a place to bury these bones;
I travel in order to find *Shilupi Yokni* for my family,
Yet there is no guide for us who must relearn *Chatah Anumpa*.

Dear Great Mother and Great Spirit, I am but a descendant of your people.
I am waiting patiently to hear your, "*Halito*" welcome us;
I travel in order to put the *shilombish* to rest,
Those who have passed and now watch over us.

Dear *Nanin Waiya*, I am a descendant of your people.
I am a Christian, and I am learner of indigenous practices.
I travel in order to put at rest all that I detest.
We are darkened-skinned children telling you, "*Chi hullo li.*"

*Translation: All is Choctaw/Chatah Anumpa:
Isht Chito means *Great Mother, the Mother Mound.*
Atuklant Illi means *the Second Death* (similar to Christian Hell, it is located west of the
Mother Mound).
Chitokaka means *Great Spirit.*
Shilup means *second shadow* or *soul* (the soul is divided into two parts).
Shilupi Yokni means *Place of light and happiness.*
Halito means *Hello.*
Shilombish means *outside shadow.*
Nanin Waiya is another name for *the Mother Mound* (more closely related to the hole that
swallowed up the holy man and place of burial).
Chi hullo li means *I love you.*

Shamir Kali Griffin

I am lines of poetry and prose with inadequate structure,
The playfulness of lyrics unspoken on bedroom tongues.
I exist quietly yet let my actions speak louder than my spoken word.
I am lyrics without a poem to belong to or a poet to hold on to.

My love is a ghost in the room only visible through the lens of hindsight.
It's emotion stuck in its ways, lingering on foreign clothes.
It is coldness that has replaced delicate warmth and tenderness.
My love is a golden-magnum wrapper covering a coal-black heart.

My heart is a thick yet carefully crafted clump of Christmas coal,
Though dark it offers eternal heat for those with affection to spark.
It is fast-sprinting marathon runner speeding past adversity.
My heart is a thick clump of dark coal becoming something valuable.

My soul is a refugee seeking sanctuary and nourishment.
It travels tirelessly to the walls of Zion.
It has suffered discrimination, acts of prejudice by its comrades.
My soul is a refugee seeking asylum from the vernacular.

My mind is Black history and Kappa Sigma diligence,
Native resilience, state-funded education, Eurocentric humiliation.
It is fed on Aristotle's rhetoric and Hippocrates's oaths yet hungry.
My mind is made full by R and B, neo soul, Lauryn Hill, and Erykah Badu.

I am lines of poetry without a poem to belong to,
Words left to linger and cultivate fertile minds.
My quiet actions speak louder than my spoken word.
I am lines of poetry without an audience to hear them.

My Prayer

Today I held hands with a homeless man;
I saw that his hands were covered in filth and sin,
Yet I did not shy away as mine were too.
With this thought, I embraced him as a brother.

"Dear God, thank you for carrying me through tribulations
Although I carry human filth and sin into your temple.
I open my heart to you, Lord, as I seek to wash these hands
Within those blessed tears your son cried for us.

Please, God, continue to watch over those whom I love;
Guide us carefully through these hit-and-run worlds.
Although many of us stay on autopilot, let us not forget
That your word is the vehicle that carries us, amen."

Today I held the hand of a woman with thin, shaking hands,
Pale hands with lack of strength or flesh to cling to them.
Yet I did not let this defer me as we are all weak in solitude,
For within fellowship under your name, we are strengthened.

Pray for Me

I am supposed to keep faith but does faith keep me
When I am disproportionately afflicted with misfortune and malady?
I ask that people pray for me, but recent news has me buried: cemetery.

I am filled with righteous, sanctified indignation
Only to suffer continuous monetary humiliation.
Contemplating selling myself to help ease financial frustration
But need to keep myself positive, unlike leading actress in *Temptation*.

I am both lost and found yet never claimed in reality
As I calm internal urges to end my own life violently.
My mind lies still for a second, and I live in the past momentarily
And become delusional laughing over past mistakes: hilarity.

I try and calm this sea of despair with time-honed meditation
But find myself succumbing to unpleasantness: suicidal ideation.
Honest to God, what is the point of this prescribed medication
When I still suffer anxiety attacks, cluster migraines, and major depression?

Bonus Chapter: Poetic Soul

The following poems were simply created for the enjoyment of readers who purchased this new edition of the book. May they offer you warmth, insight, humor, and understanding.

The color of this chapter is the color white. White may represent beginnings, cleanliness, and purity; however, using the light spectrum, white is a combination of all possible colors. This final chapter encompasses a variety of poems that could easily fit into other sections, but it is a combination of the various colors and themes that both this final chapter and the book are constructed from. Many of these love poems were inspired by someone who entered my life on December 18, 2014.

The Truth

Crypts, Bloods, Norteños, Surreños, and Boarder Brothers
Focus on small differences and kill another.
They isolate and destroy indiscriminately,
Not knowing they play into the game of white supremacy.

They are knights in the game of neocolonialism,
As the kings market it to the pawns as friendly globalism.
We are bought and sold a life like that of slaves on the sale block
As we become bound by bondage again in a prison cellblock.

Activists like rooks charge forward in one direction,
Yet voices are ignored as youth prefer to follow One Direction.
We are under the foot of an educational embargo
As we accept what is fed to us, remaining ignorant, refusing to know.

The queens are the intellectual elites who are free to navigate
Although they are aware of the system that they are bound by fate.
They move straight forward and if need be diagonally,
Like the aforementioned knights trying not to be a bagged body.

You are the bishop, who with knowledge and ability may preach,
Taking fruit from this poem to help expand your reach.
Will you choose to be knowledgeable of the situation and remedy this infliction?
Will you become blocked by pawns and assassinated by the next generation?

4:00 a.m. Monotony (Soiled Pillow Talk)

The bitterness of one-night stands,
That void filled with strangers' hands.
Eyelashes flutter over stained bedsheets
As familiar scenes are relived, and they weep.

Memories that sleep quietly on my skin
As a new presence is welcomed in.
Varying shades of soul invite wandering lips
As tired eyes hide under welcoming hips.

This is the anthem of soiled pillow talk,
Moments spent in bed, chastity not on Lock.
A routine founded on naivety in momentary comfort,
One soured at the moment of departure.

Amor (Hecho de Mano)

En la mañana antes que nos levantamos mi espíritu desparece,
Y mi cuerpo duerme esperando para conocerte.
Mientras que te despartas, me curas de mi enfermedad
Con tu amor simpático hecho de mano.

En la tarde antes de vamos a trabajar,
Mi corazón muere y no puedo caminar,
Mientras que me abracas, me llenas con alegría.
Con tu amor fuerte hecho de mano.

En la noche cuando el día desagua mi energía,
Y mis manos pierdan su poder, me das vida,
Mientras que me besas, me enseñas de todo
Con tu amor sabio hecho de mano.

Absolution

I want to express myself in something more divine than testimony
As I speak in tongues that excite you in forbidden ways, Deuteronomy!
We are both sinners who cannot learn how to forgive;
For both greed and lust help fuel this sin that now lives.

I divide your soaking-wet body like Moses did the sea
Though, like Noah, you had two of each animal beside you nightly.
We are covered in a multitude of sins, ones that love cannot remedy.
So I rest inside of you like Jonah and the Whale as we commit blasphemy.

You are David, and I am the heathen known as Goliath
As we scribe biblical narratives on each other's skin: hieroglyph.
This is not the love of first Corinthians thirteen, a spiritual gift.
It is the tampered sin that helped turn Sodom into a Monolith.

Sins become embedded into our souls waiting for this absolution,
Waiting for the brilliance of love to remove this spiritual pollution.
We attempt to make love hoping it will "Cover a multitude of sins,"
Yet our love differs from that found in first Corinthians.

We walk quietly under the luminous, divine countenance
As we let go of sin to be filled with spiritual nourishment.
Two individuals once cloaked in sin and smothered in guilt
Lose individuality and absolve one another as barriers are killed.

Expiration Date

What happens to leftover love held past its expiration date?
Does the sweetness sour and spoil, turning it into hate?
To love someone that stopped loving is both selfish and masochistic,
The type of emotional turmoil that pampers suicide statistics.

Time kisses the sealed contents of an empty container,
And there is no love left to make with the nonexistent remainder.
Souls unravel quietly on their own time and emotion rots.
Love is sacrificed early on like Black guys in horror plots!

Faces

Memories, faces, and scents disguised as possibilities without faces
Are harmonizing soulless ballads as my mind crosses into strange places.
Faces that appear as strangers in the hall with too much familiarity,
Ones that speak only in empty promises only filled with melancholy.

They are nameless figures with facts attached to them,
Ones that become erased as they dwell in sin.

I am a victim of the "whatever floats your boat" mentality
As they feast on my flesh being filled momentarily.
Legs, arms, and celibacy put under lock and key,
One that has been broken and appears flimsy.

They are familiar strangers who gather in the dark corridors of my mind,
That bring cacophony that can only be silenced with a glass of wine.

Memories, faces, and scents disguised as fulfillment without form,
Created from broken promises, sullied words, and projections of porn.
Faces that appear as strangers in the hall, who survive on NSA hookups
Only to lose their last few moments on avoided STD checkups.

Runaway

Loud roars force you out of the place you called home
As emotions fuel feet to move to a place you can be alone.
Let my embrace be the warmth that makes the streets tolerable
As I slide inside to give you pleasure unbearable.

Quiet whispers assure you of this place we called Ours
As you hide yourself inside this world and rest for hours.
Let strong hands be the support that your soul needs
As I plow you though planting a seed.

I See

I see the curiosity of the world reflected in your eyes,
The radiance of hope that pours over you, my prize.
Yo veo un futuro promisorio por delante
Y no puedo pensar mas que, "Yo quiero conocerte!"

You see in me my happiness, sorrow, and resentment,
Yet you embrace them all with a sanctified commitment.
Tu ves en mi un pasado lleno de dolor,
Y como puedes eliminar todo con amor!

Take Time

I want to feel, taste, and explore the vast richness of your entirety,
To understand the depth of your essence that defies antiquity.
Before I can take a step forward, I think it's best we take time
As to avoid infatuation or inebriation from fruit distilled, wine.

I want to create, destroy, and appreciate the delicacies you hide
As I let hormones and present events take me on this ride.
Before I can let my senses become indulgent with yours,
I need to reaffirm that we desire more than intercourse.

I want to become filled, insane, and conquered by your intellect,
To harmonize myself with your circadian rhythms while you slept.
Before I can undress my very soul and morality in front of you,
To make sure you are attracted to more than this fleeting view.

(All of these new love poems are dedicated to my new love, TMG.)

Author's Note

My purpose in writing this final anthology titled *Identity in Shades* is to offer much more to the world than I can in my daily life. To give words to those who have become speechless and to those who have been marginalized and oppressed. To give comfort and feelings of solidarity to those who feel isolated from their communities or from within their communities. To give warmth and authenticity in a cold world that seeks similarity and conformity. To help build up those who have lost a foundation, and more importantly, to offer a good read to those seeking one. With this statement, I present you with my *Identity in Shades*.

Thanks and Recognition

I would like to give thanks to my brothers in the Omicron Mu chapter of the Kappa Sigma fraternity, to my fellow officers in the Psi Chi International Honor Society, and to my family. I would like to give further honor and gratitude to those members of the Decameron Foundation and Joushya Cole. Without any of you present, I would not be who I am today—whether that is a good thing, you can decide.

Made in United States
North Haven, CT
19 September 2023

41740394R00109